Truth Eternal

Truth Eternal

Six Essential Doctrinal Works
Every Latter-day Saint Should Know

Compiled and annotated by Jack M. Lyon

TEMPLE HILL

ISBN 1-60096-518-0

Published by Temple Hill Books, an imprint of The Editorium.

Temple Hill Books™, the Temple Hill Books logo, and The Editorium™ are trademarks of The Editorium, LLC, which is not affiliated with The Church of Jesus Christ of Latter-day Saints.

The Editorium, LLC
West Valley City, UT 84128
www.templehillbooks.com
templehill@editorium.com

Contents

Publisher's Preface

"This is life eternal, that they might know thee the only true God, and Jesus Christ, whom thou hast sent." (John 17:3.)

President Gordon B. Hinckley once observed, "Great indeed is our debt to [Joseph Smith]. . . . It was he who brought us a true knowledge of God, the Eternal Father, and His Risen Son, the Lord Jesus Christ."[1]

President Brigham Young recalled, "When I first heard [Joseph Smith] preach, he brought heaven and earth together, and all the priests of the day could not tell me anything correct about heaven, hell, God, angels, nor devils; they were as blind as Egyptian darkness. When I saw Joseph Smith, he took heaven, figuratively speaking, . . . and opened up in plainness and simplicity the things of God, and that is the beauty of his mission."[2]

Some of these "things of God" are found in the Book of Mormon, the Doctrine and Covenants, and the Pearl of Great Price. Others are found in later revelations to the leaders of the Church, and these, too, are scripture, even though they are not part of the official LDS canon. As the Lord said, "Whatsoever [my servants] shall speak when moved upon by the Holy Ghost shall be scripture, shall be the will of the Lord, shall be the mind of the Lord, shall be the word of the Lord, shall be the voice of the Lord, and the power of God unto salvation." (D&C 68:4.)

---

1. *Ensign*, December 1997, 2.
2. *Discourses of Brigham Young*, sel. John A. Widtsoe (Salt Lake City: Deseret Book, 1941), 458.

At a symposium on the New Testament on August 15–17, 1984, at Brigham Young University, Provo, Utah, Elder Bruce R. McConkie, of the Quorum of the Twelve Apostles, gave a landmark address titled "The Bible, a Sealed Book." In it he noted:

> We should be aware that there are approved and inspired writings that are not in the standard works. *These writings also are true* and should be used along with the scriptures themselves in learning and teaching the gospel. Next to the standard works, five of the greatest documents in our literature are—
>
> 1. The "Wentworth Letter."[3] Written by the Prophet Joseph Smith, it contains an account of the coming forth of the Book of Mormon, of the ancient inhabitants of the Americas, of the organization of the Church in this dispensation, and of the persecutions suffered by the early Latter-day Saints. The thirteen Articles of Faith are part of this letter.
>
> 2. *Lectures on Faith.* These lectures were prepared by and under the direction of the Prophet Joseph Smith and were taught by him and by others in the School of the Prophets. The Prophet said they embraced "the important doctrine[s] of salvation."[4]
>
> 3. *The Father and the Son: A Doctrinal Exposition by the First Presidency and the Twelve.*[5] This exposition sets forth the status and relationship of the Father and the Son, shows those ways in which Christ is the Father, and through its various recitations lays to rest the false and heretical view that Adam is our Father and our God.
>
> 4. The "King Follett Sermon" and the "Sermon in the Grove."[6] These two sermons, one in thought and content,

---

3. See *History of the Church*, 7 vols., 2d ed. rev., ed. B. H. Roberts (Salt Lake City: The Church of Jesus Christ of Latter-day Saints, 1932-51), 4:535–41.

4. Preface to D&C 1835 ed.; reprint, Independence, Mo.: Herald House, 1971

5. See James R. Clark, comp., *Messages of the First Presidency of the The Church of Jesus Christ of Latter-day Saints*, 6 vols. [Salt Lake City: Bookcraft, 1965–75], 5:26–34; see also 5:23–25. Also published in the *Ensign*, April 2002, 13.

6. See *History of the Church*, 6:302–17; 6:473–79.

set forth the doctrine of the plurality of Gods and of becoming joint heirs with Christ. They show that man may become as his Maker and reign in celestial exaltation forever.

5. "The Origin of Man," by the First Presidency of the Church.[7] This inspired writing sets forth the official position of the Church on the origin of man.

In recent years, members of The Church of Jesus Christ of Latter-day Saints have rightly placed increasing emphasis on the role of the Savior and his atonement in the plan of salvation. Unfortunately, in an effort to placate other churches, some members have gone further, seeking to lay aside some of the Church's most important and distinctive doctrines as taught in the documents mentioned by Elder McConkie. These include the truths that God was once a man, that man may become like God, and that we are children of a Heavenly Mother as well as a Heavenly Father. It is one thing to build bridges with others; it is another to burn our own bridges behind us. Perhaps we would do better to follow the example of the Prophet Joseph.

In 1839 Joseph Smith, Sidney Rigdon, and others traveled to Washington, D.C., to present their petitions for redress for the crimes committed against them by the Missourians. During the trip, they were invited to speak to about three thousand people in Philadelphia. President Rigdon addressed the group first. In an effort to avoid confrontation, he used Bible references in an attempt to prove that the Church was true, avoiding any reference to the visions and revelations of the Restoration. The Prophet was visibly disappointed at Sidney's defense. Parley P. Pratt observed that the Prophet could barely sit still:

> When [Sidney Rigdon] was through, brother Joseph arose like a lion about to roar; and being full of the Holy Ghost, spoke in great power, bearing testimony of the visions he had seen, the ministering of angels which he had

---

7. See Clark, *Messages of the First Presidency*, 4:200–206; see also 4:199. Also published in the *Ensign*, Feb. 2002, 26.

enjoyed; and how he had found the plates of the Book of Mormon, and translated them by the gift and power of God. He commenced by saying: "If nobody else had the courage to testify . . . of so glorious a record, he felt to do it in justice to the people, and leave the event to God."

The entire congregation was astounded; electrified, as it were, and overwhelmed with the sense of truth and power by which he spoke, and the wonders which he related. A lasting impression was made; many souls were gathered into the fold. And I bear witness, that he, by his faithful and powerful testimony, cleared his garments of their blood.[8]

Like Brother Joseph, we should not be afraid to teach the precious truths revealed as part of the restoration of the gospel, even if they make us unpopular. "I am not ashamed of the gospel of Christ." (Romans 1:16.)

Some find it convenient to ignore the teachings of Joseph Smith and Brigham Young, with the admonition that we are to "look to the living oracles," the current leaders of the Church. Of course we are to look to the living oracles, but that does not mean that the dead ones should be forgotten or that their inspired teachings are no longer valid. The test of validity is truth, which we may know for ourselves by the revelations of the Holy Ghost.

This book, *Truth Eternal,* includes the foundational documents listed by Elder McConkie, along with a few other works that teach the most glorious truths of the Restoration—which, in fact, *are* the "true knowledge of God" mentioned by President Hinckley. These truths must not be lost or glossed over, for they, along with the Atonement, are at the very core of the plan of salvation, revealing the fundamental meaning of life and the transcendent purpose of our Heavenly Father's work: "to bring to pass the immortality and eternal life of man." (Moses 1:39.)

---

8. Parley P. Pratt, *Autobiography of Parley P. Pratt* [Salt Lake City: Deseret Book, 1938], 298–99.

The King Follett Discourse

Joseph Smith

President Joseph Smith delivered the following discourse[1] before about twenty thousand Saints at the April General Conference of the Church, 1844, being the funeral sermon of Elder King Follett. Reported by Willard Richards, Wilford Woodruff, Thomas Bullock, and William Clayton.

Beloved Saints: I will call [for] the attention of this congregation while I address you on the subject of the dead. The decease of our beloved brother, Elder King Follett, who was crushed in a well by the falling of a tub of rock has more immediately led me to this subject. I have been requested to speak by his friends and

---

1. The version included here was taken from the Prophet's *History of the Church* and was published by the Church as part of the "Classics in Mormon Thought" series in the *Ensign* in April and May of 1971. It was reconstructed from the longhand notes of Thomas Bullock, William Clayton, Willard Richards, and Wilford Woodruff, who were present when the address was given. The *History of the Church* explains, "This was not a stenographic report, but a carefully and skillfully prepared one made by these men, who were trained in reporting and taking notes. Evidently, there are some imperfections in the report and some thoughts expressed by the Prophet which were not fully rounded out and made complete." A newly amalgamated version was published in *BYU Studies,* Winter 1978, 193, available online at http://tinyurl.com/opvhm. The separate accounts are available in Donald Q. Cannon and Larry E. Dahl, *The Prophet Joseph Smith's King Follett Discourse: A Six-Column Comparison of Original Notes and Amalgamations* (Provo: Religious Studies Center, Brighm Young University, 1983). They are also available online at http://www.boap.org/LDS/Parallel/1844/7Apr44.html.

1

relatives, but inasmuch as there are a great many in this congregation who live in this city as well as elsewhere, who have lost friends, I feel disposed to speak on the subject in general, and offer you my ideas, so far as I have ability, and so far as I shall be inspired by the Holy Spirit to dwell on this subject.

I want your prayers and faith that I may have the instruction of Almighty God and the gift of the Holy Ghost, so that I may set forth things that are true and which can be easily comprehended by you, and that the testimony may carry conviction to your hearts and minds of the truth of what I shall say. Pray that the Lord may strengthen my lungs, stay the winds, and let the prayers of the Saints to heaven appear, that they may enter into the ears of the Lord of Sabaoth, for the effectual prayers of the righteous avail much. There is strength here, and I verily believe that your prayers will be heard.

Before I enter fully into the investigation of the subject which is lying before me, I wish to pave the way and bring up the subject from the beginning, that you may understand it. I will make a few preliminaries, in order that you may understand the subject when I come to it. I do not calculate or intend to please your ears with superfluity of words or oratory, or with much learning; but I calculate [intend] to edify you with the simple truths from heaven.

The Character of God

In the first place, I wish to go back to the beginning—to the morn of creation. There is the starting point for us to look to, in order to understand and be fully acquainted with the mind, purposes and decrees of the Great Eloheim, who sits in yonder heavens as he did at the creation of the world. It is necessary for us to have an understanding of God himself in the beginning. If we start right, it is easy to go right all the time; but if we start wrong we may go wrong, and it will be a hard matter to get right.

There are but a very few beings in the world who understand rightly the character of God. The great majority of mankind do not comprehend anything, either that which is past, or that

2

which is to come, as it respects their relationship to God. They do not know, neither do they understand the nature of that relationship; and consequently they know but little above the brute beast, or more than to eat, drink and sleep. This is all man knows about God and His existence, unless it is given by the inspiration of the Almighty.

If a man learns nothing more than to eat, drink and sleep, and does not comprehend any of the designs of God, the beast comprehends the same things. It eats, drinks, sleeps, and knows nothing more about God; yet it knows as much as we, unless we are able to comprehend by the inspiration of Almighty God. If men do not comprehend the character of God, they do not comprehend themselves. I want to go back to the beginning, and so lift your minds into more lofty spheres and a more exalted understanding than what the human mind generally aspires to.

I want to ask this congregation, every man, woman and child, to answer the question in their own hearts, what kind of a being God is? Ask yourselves; turn your thoughts into your hearts, and say if any of you have seen, heard, or communed with Him? This is a question that may occupy your attention for a long time. I again repeat the question—What kind of being is God? Does any man or woman know? Have any of you seen Him, heard Him, or communed with Him? Here is the question that will, peradventure, from this time henceforth occupy your attention. The scriptures inform us that "this is life eternal, that they might know thee the only true God, and Jesus Christ, whom thou hast sent." (John 17:3.)

If any man does not know God, and inquires what kind of a being He is—if he will search diligently his own heart—if the declaration of Jesus and the apostles be true, he will realize that he has not eternal life; for there can be eternal life on no other principle.

My first object is to find out the character of the only wise and true God, and what kind of a being He is; and if I am so fortunate as to be the man to comprehend God, and explain or convey the principles to your hearts, so that the Spirit seals them upon you, then let every man and woman henceforth sit in silence, put their hands on their mouths, and never lift their hands or voices, or say anything against the man of God or the servants of God again. But if I fail to do it, it becomes my duty to renounce all further pretensions to revelations and inspirations, or to be a prophet; and I should be like the rest of the world—a false teacher, be hailed as a friend, and no man would seek my life. But if all religious teachers were honest enough to renounce their pretensions to godliness when their ignorance of the knowledge of God is made manifest, they will all be as badly off as I am, at any rate; and you might just as well take the lives of other false teachers as that of mine. If any man is authorized to take away my life because he thinks and says I am a false teacher, then, upon the same principle, we should be justified in taking away the life of every false teacher, and where would be the end of blood? And who would not be the sufferer?[2]

THE PRIVILEGE OF RELIGIOUS FREEDOM

But meddle not with any man for his religion: all governments ought to permit every man to enjoy his religion unmolested. No man is authorized to take away life in consequence of difference of religion, which all laws and governments ought to tolerate and protect, right or wrong. Every man has a natural, and, in our country, a constitutional right to be a false prophet, as well as a true prophet. If I show, verily, that I have the truth of God, and show that ninety-nine out of every hundred professing religious ministers are false teachers, having no authority, while they pretend to hold the keys of God's kingdom on earth, and was to kill them because they are false teachers, it would deluge the whole world with blood.

I will prove that the world is wrong, by showing what God is. I am going to inquire after God; for I want you all to know Him, and to be familiar with Him; and if I am bringing you to

---

2. This discourse was given just two months before the Prophet's murder. During this time the enemies of the Church were extremely active, and the Prophet undoubtedly anticipated the coming events that would culminate in his death.

4

a knowledge of Him, all persecutions against me ought to cease. You will then know that I am His servant; for I speak as one having authority.

GOD AN EXALTED MAN

I will go back to the beginning before the world was, to show what kind of a being God is. What sort of a being was God in the beginning? Open your ears and hear, all ye ends of the earth, for I am going to prove it to you by the Bible, and to tell you the designs of God in relation to the human race, and why He interferes with the affairs of man.

God himself was once as we are now, and is an exalted man,[3] and sits enthroned in yonder heavens! That is the great secret. If the veil were rent today, and the great God who holds this world in its orbit, and who upholds all worlds and all things by His power, was to make himself visible—I say, if you were to see him today, you would see him like a man in form—like yourselves in all the person, image, and very form as a man; for Adam was created in the very fashion, image and likeness of God, and received instruction from, and walked, talked and conversed with Him, as one man talks and communes with another.[4]

------

3. Critics of the Church claim that this doctrine shows that the Latter-day Saints worship a "different Jesus" than they do. In actuality, this claim is true, for the critics worship the bodiless, passionless, nonexistent god of the Greek philosphers as adopted by the Council of Nicea in 325 A.D.—a god who can "neither see, nor hear, nor eat, nor smell." (Deuteronmy 4:28.) As the Lord himself told young Joseph in the First Vision, "They teach for doctrines the commandments of men." (Joseph Smith–History 1:19.) Latter-day Saints, in contrast, worship the God of the Bible, who walked in the garden of Eden, talked with Moses face to face, and ate fish and honeycomb at the Sea of Galilee. He is the true and *living* God of Abraham, Isaac, and Jacob—the great Jehovah, the resurrected Lord, who has revealed anew his existence and his nature in these last days of the world. "Ye worship ye know not what: we know what we worship." (John 4:22; see D&C 93:19.)

4. This distinctive and important doctrine is taught on page 40 of the Church's 2007 priesthood and Relief Society lesson manual, *Teachings of Presidents of the Church: Joseph Smith.* It was also taught by the First Presidency in "The Origin of Man," included in this book: "God Himself is an exalted man, perfected, enthroned, and supreme."

In order to understand the subject of the dead, for consolation of those who mourn for the loss of their friends, it is necessary we should understand the character and being of God and how He came to be so; for I am going to tell you how God came to be God. We have imagined and supposed that God was God from all eternity. I will refute that idea, and take away the veil, so that you may see.

These ideas are incomprehensible to some, but they are simple. It is the first principle of the gospel to know for a certainty the character of God, and to know that we may converse with Him as one man converses with another, and that He was once a man like us; yea, that God himself, the Father of us all, dwelt on an earth, the same as Jesus Christ Himself did; and I will show it from the Bible.

Eternal Life to Know God and Jesus Christ

I wish I was in a suitable place to tell it, and that I had the trump of an archangel, so that I could tell the story in such a manner that persecution would cease forever. What did Jesus say? (Mark it, Elder Rigdon!) The scriptures inform us that Jesus said, as the Father hath power in himself, even so hath the Son power—to do what? Why, what the Father did. The answer is obvious—in a manner to lay down his body and take it up again. Jesus, what are you going to do? To lay down my life as my Father did, and take it up again. Do you believe it? If you do not believe it you do not believe the Bible. The scriptures say it, and I defy all the learning and wisdom and all the combined powers of earth and hell together to refute it. Here, then, is eternal life—to know the only wise and true God; and you have got to learn how to be gods yourselves, and to be kings and priests to God, the same as all gods have done before you, namely, by going from one small degree to another, and from a small capacity to a great one; from grace to grace, from exaltation to exaltation, until you attain to the resurrection of the dead, and are able to dwell in everlasting burnings, and to sit in glory, as do those who sit enthroned in everlasting power. And I want you to know that

God, in the last days, while certain individuals are proclaiming His name, is not trifling with you or me.

THE RIGHTEOUS TO DWELL IN EVERLASTING BURNINGS

These are the first principles of consolation. How consoling to the mourners when they are called to part with a husband, wife, father, mother, child, or dear relative, to know that, although the earthly tabernacle is laid down and dissolved, they shall rise again to dwell in everlasting burnings in immortal glory, not to sorrow, suffer, or die any more, but they shall be heirs of God and joint heirs with Jesus Christ. What is it? To inherit the same power, the same glory and the same exaltation, until you arrive at the station of a god, and ascend the throne of eternal power, the same as those who have gone before. What did Jesus do? Why, I do the things I saw my Father do when worlds came rolling into existence. My Father worked out His kingdom with fear and trembling, and I must do the same; and when I get my kingdom, I shall present it to My Father, so that He may obtain kingdom upon kingdom, and it will exalt Him in glory. He will then take a higher exaltation, and I will take His place, and thereby become exalted myself. So that Jesus treads in the tracks of His Father, and inherits what God did before; and God is thus glorified and exalted in the salvation and exaltation of all His children. It is plain beyond disputation, and you thus learn some of the first principles of the gospel, about which so much hath been said.

When you climb up a ladder, you must begin at the bottom, and ascend step by step, until you arrive at the top; and so it is with the principles of the gospel—you must begin with the first, and go on until you learn all the principles of exaltation. But it will be a great while after you have passed through the veil before you will have learned them. It is not all to be comprehended in this world; it will be a great work to learn our salvation and exaltation even beyond the grave. I suppose I am not allowed to go into an investigation of anything that is not contained in the Bible. If I do, I think there are so many over-wise men here that they would cry "treason" and put me to death. So I will go to the old Bible and turn commentator today.

I shall comment on the very first Hebrew word in the Bible; I will make a comment on the very first sentence of the history of creation in the Bible—*Berosheit*. I want to analyze the word. *Baith*—in, by, through, and everything else. *Rosh*—the head, *Sheit*—grammatical termination. When the inspired man wrote it, he did not put the baith there. An old Jew without any authority added the word; he thought it too bad to begin to talk about the head! It read first, "The head one of the Gods brought forth the Gods." That is the true meaning of the words. *Baurau* signifies to bring forth. If you do not believe it, you do not believe the learned man of God. Learned men can teach you no more than what I have told you. Thus the head God brought forth the Gods in the grand council.

I will transpose and simplify it in the English language. Oh, ye lawyers, ye doctors, and ye priests, who have persecuted me, I want to let you know that the Holy Ghost knows something as well as you do. The head God called together the Gods and sat in grand council to bring forth the world. The grand councilors sat at the head in yonder heavens and contemplated the creation of the worlds which were created at the time. When I say doctors and lawyers, I mean the doctors and lawyers of the scriptures. I have done so hitherto without explanation, to let the lawyers flutter and everybody laugh at them. Some learned doctors might take a notion to say the scriptures say thus and so; and we must believe the scriptures; they are not to be altered. But I am going to show you an error in them.

I have an old edition of the New Testament in the Latin, Hebrew, German and Greek languages. I have been reading the German, and find it to be the most [nearly] correct translation, and to correspond nearest to the revelations which God has given to me for the last fourteen years. It tells about Jacobus, the son of Zebedee. It means Jacob. In the English New Testament it is translated James. Now, if Jacob had the keys, you might talk about James through all eternity and never get the keys. In the 21st [verse] of the fourth chapter of Matthew, my old German edition gives the word Jacob instead of James.

The doctors (I mean doctors of law, not physic) say, "If you preach anything not according to the Bible, we will cry treason." How can we escape the damnation of hell, except God be with us and reveal to us? Men bind us with chains. The Latin says Jacobus, which means Jacob; the Hebrew says Jacob, the Greek says Jacob and the German says Jacob, here we have the testimony of four against one. I thank God that I have got this old book; but I thank him more for the gift of the Holy Ghost. I have got the oldest book in the world; but I have got the oldest book in my heart, even the gift of the Holy Ghost. I have all the four Testaments. Come here, ye learned men, and read, if you can. I should not have introduced this testimony, were it not to back up the word *rosh*—the head, the Father of the Gods. I should not have brought it up, only to show that I am right.

A COUNCIL OF THE GODS

In the beginning, the head of the Gods called a council of the Gods; and they came together and concocted [prepared] a plan to create the world and people it. When we begin to learn this way, we begin to learn the only true God, and what kind of a being we have got to worship. Having a knowledge of God, we begin to know how to approach Him, and how to ask so as to receive an answer.

When we understand the character of God, and know how to come to Him, he begins to unfold the heavens to us, and to tell us all about it. When we are ready to come to him, he is ready to come to us.

Now, I ask all who hear me, why the learned men who are preaching salvation, say that God created the heavens and the earth out of nothing? The reason is, that they are unlearned in the things of God, and have not the gift of the Holy Ghost; they account it blasphemy in any one to contradict their idea. If you tell them that God made the world out of something, they will call you a fool. But I am learned, and know more than all the world put together. The Holy Ghost does, anyhow, and he is within me, and comprehends more than all the world; and I will associate myself with him.

MEANING OF THE WORD "CREATE"

You ask the learned doctors why they say the world was made out of nothing, and they will answer, "Doesn't the Bible say he *created* the world?" And they infer, from the word create, that it must have been made out of nothing. Now, the word create came from the word *baurau*, which does not mean to create out of nothing; it means to organize; the same as a man would organize materials and build a ship. Hence we infer that God had materials to organize the world out of chaos—chaotic matter, which is element, and in which dwells all the glory. Element had an existence from the time He had. The pure principles of element are principles which can never be destroyed; they may be organized and re-organized, but not destroyed. They had no beginning and can have no end.

THE IMMORTAL INTELLIGENCE

I have another subject to dwell upon, which is calculated to exalt man; but it is impossible for me to say much on this subject. I shall therefore just touch upon it, for time will not permit me to say all. It is associated with the subject of the resurrection of the dead—namely, the soul—the mind of man—the immortal spirit. Where did it come from? All learned men and doctors of divinity say that God created it in the beginning; but it is not so: the very idea lessens man in my estimation. I do not believe the doctrine; I know better. Hear it, all ye ends of the world; for God has told me so; and if you don't believe me, it will not make the truth without effect. I will make a man appear a fool before I get through; if he does not believe it. I am going to tell of things more noble.

We say that God Himself is a self-existing being. Who told you so? It is correct enough; but how did it get into your heads? Who told you that man did not exist in like manner upon the same principles? Man does exist upon the same principles. God made a tabernacle and put a spirit into it, and it became a living soul. (Refers to the Bible.) How does it read in the Hebrew? It does not say in the Hebrew that God created the spirit of man. It

10

says, "God made man out of the earth and put into him Adam's spirit, and so became a living body."

The mind or the intelligence which man possesses is co-equal[5] with God himself.[6] I know that my testimony is true; hence, when I talk to these mourners, what have they lost? Their relatives and friends are only separated from their bodies for a short season: their spirits which existed with God have left the tabernacle of clay only for a little moment, as it were; and they now exist in a place where they converse together the same as we do on the earth.

I am dwelling on the immortality of the spirit of man. Is it logical to say that the intelligence of spirits is immortal, and yet that it has a beginning? The intelligence of spirits had no beginning, neither will it have an end. That is good logic. That which has a beginning may have an end. There never was a time when there were not spirits; for they are co-equal with our Father in heaven.

I want to reason more on the spirit of man; for I am dwelling on the body and spirit of man—on the subject of the dead. I take my ring from my finger and liken it unto the mind of man—the immortal part, because it had no beginning. Suppose you cut it in two; then it has a beginning and an end; but join it again, and it continues one eternal round. So with the spirit of man. As the Lord liveth, if it had a beginning, it will have an end. All the fools and learned and wise men from the beginning of creation, who say that the spirit of man had a beginning, prove that it must have an end; and if that doctrine is true, then the doctrine of annihilation would be true. But if I am right, I might with boldness proclaim from the housetops that God never had the power to create the spirit of man at all. God himself could not create himself.

---

5. The Prophet may have meant "coeval" (or perhaps his scribes misheard). The word means "of the same or equal age, antiquity, or duration." (In *History of the Church*, B. H. Roberts added a note that "co-eternal" was meant.)

6. As the Lord teaches in D&C 93:29, "Man was also in the beginning with God. Intelligence, or the light of truth, was not created or made, neither indeed can be."

Intelligence is eternal and exists upon a self-existent principle. It is a spirit from age to age and there is no creation about it. All the minds and spirits that God ever sent into the world are susceptible of enlargement.

The first principles of man are self-existent with God. God himself, finding he was in the midst of spirits and glory, because he was more intelligent, saw proper to institute laws whereby the rest could have a privilege to advance like himself. The relationship we have with God places us in a situation to advance in knowledge. He has power to institute laws to instruct the weaker intelligences, that they may be exalted with Himself, so that they might have one glory upon another, and all that knowledge, power, glory, and intelligence, which is requisite in order to save them in the world of spirits.

This is good doctrine. It tastes good. I can taste the principles of eternal life, and so can you. They are given to me by the revelations of Jesus Christ; and I know that when I tell you these words of eternal life as they are given to me, you taste them, and I know that you believe them. You say honey is sweet, and so do I. I can also taste the spirit of eternal life. I know that it is good; and when I tell you of these things which were given me by inspiration of the Holy Spirit, you are bound to receive them as sweet, and rejoice more and more.

THE RELATION OF MAN TO GOD

I want to talk more of the relation of man to God. I will open your eyes in relation to the dead. All things whatsoever God in his infinite wisdom has seen fit and proper to reveal to us, while we are dwelling in mortality, in regard to our mortal bodies, are revealed to us in the abstract, and independent of affinity of this mortal tabernacle, but are revealed to our spirits precisely as though we had no bodies at all; and those revelations which will save our spirits will save our bodies. God reveals them to us in view of no eternal dissolution of the body, or tabernacle. Hence the responsibility, the awful responsibility, that rests upon us in relation to our dead; for all the spirits who have not obeyed

12

the Gospel in the flesh must either obey it in the spirit or be damned. Solemn thought!—dreadful thought! Is there nothing to be done?—no preparation—no salvation for our fathers and friends who have died without having had the opportunity to obey the decrees of the Son of Man? Would to God that I had forty days and nights in which to tell you all! I would let you know that I am not a "fallen prophet."

OUR GREATEST RESPONSIBILITY

What promises are made in relation to the subject of the salvation of the dead? and what kind of characters are those who can be saved, although their bodies are mouldering and decaying in the grave? When His commandments teach us, it is in view of eternity; for we are looked upon by God as though we were in eternity; God dwells in eternity, and does not view things as we do.

The greatest responsibility in this world that God has laid upon us is to seek after our dead. The apostle says, "They without us cannot be made perfect"; for it is necessary that the sealing power should be in our hands to seal our children and our dead for the fulness of the dispensation of times—a dispensation to meet the promises made by Jesus Christ before the foundation of the world for the salvation of man.

Now, I will speak of them. I will meet Paul half way. I say to you, Paul, you cannot be perfect without us. It is necessary that those who are going before and those who come after us should have salvation in common with us; and thus hath God made it obligatory upon man. Hence, God said, "I will send you Elijah the prophet before the coming of the great and dreadful day of the Lord: he shall turn the heart of the fathers to the children, and the heart of the children to their fathers, lest I come and smite the earth with a curse."

THE UNPARDONABLE SIN

I have a declaration to make as to the provisions which God hath made to suit the conditions of man—made from before the foundation of the world. What has Jesus said? All sins, and all blasphemies, and every transgression, except one, that man can be guilty of, may be forgiven; and there is a salvation for all men, either in this world or the world to come, who have not committed the unpardonable sin, there being a provision either in this world or the world of spirits. Hence God hath made a provision that every spirit in the eternal world can be ferreted out and saved unless he has committed that unpardonable sin which cannot be remitted to him either in this world or the world of spirits. God has wrought out a salvation for all men, unless they have committed a certain sin; and every man who has a friend in the eternal world can save him, unless he has committed the unpardonable sin. And so you can see how far you can be a savior.

A man cannot commit the unpardonable sin after the dissolution of the body, and there is a way possible for escape. Knowledge saves a man; and in the world of spirits no man can be exalted but by knowledge. So long as a man will not give heed to the commandments, he must abide without salvation. If a man has knowledge, he can be saved; although, if he has been guilty of great sins, he will be punished for them. But when he consents to obey the gospel, whether here or in the world of spirits, he is saved.

A man is his own tormentor and his own condemner. Hence the saying, They shall go into the lake that burns with fire and brimstone. The torment of disappointment in the mind is as exquisite as a lake burning with fire and brimstone. I say, so is the torment of man.

I know the scriptures and understand them. I said, no man can commit the unpardonable sin after the dissolution of the body, nor in this life, until he receives the Holy Ghost; but they must do it in this world. Hence the salvation of Jesus Christ was wrought out for all men, in order to triumph over the devil; for if it did not catch him in one place, it would in another; for he stood up as a Savior. All will suffer until they obey Christ himself.

The contention in heaven was—Jesus said there would be certain souls that would not be saved; and the devil said he would save them all, and laid his plans before the grand council, who gave their vote in favor of Jesus Christ. So the devil rose up in rebellion against God, and was cast down, with all who put up their heads for him. (Book of Moses—Pearl of Great Price, Ch. 4:1–4; Book of Abraham, Ch. 3:23–28.)

THE FORGIVENESS OF SINS

All sins shall be forgiven, except the sin against the Holy Ghost; for Jesus will save all except the sons of perdition. What must a man do to commit the unpardonable sin? He must receive the Holy Ghost, have the heavens opened unto him, and know God, and then sin against him. After a man has sinned against the Holy Ghost, there is no repentance for him. He has got to say that the sun does not shine while he sees it; he has got to deny Jesus Christ when the heavens have been opened unto him, and to deny the plan of salvation with his eyes open to the truth of it; and from that time he begins to be an enemy. This is the case with many apostates of The Church of Jesus Christ of Latter-day Saints.

When a man begins to be an enemy to this work, he hunts me, he seeks to kill me, and never ceases to thirst for my blood. He gets the spirit of the devil—the same spirit that sins against the Holy Ghost. You cannot save such persons; you cannot bring them to repentance; they make open war, like the devil, and awful is the consequence.

I advise all of you to be careful what you do, or you may by-and-by find out that you have been deceived. Stay yourselves; do not give way; don't make any hasty moves, you may be saved. If a spirit of bitterness is in you, don't be in haste. You may say, that man is a sinner. Well, if he repents, he shall be forgiven. Be cautious: await. When you find a spirit that wants bloodshed,—murder, the same is not of God, but is of the devil. Out of the abundance of the heart of man the mouth speaketh.

The best men bring forth the best works. The man who tells you words of life is the man who can save you. I warn you against all evil characters who sin against the Holy Ghost; for there is no redemption for them in this world nor in the world to come.

I could go back and trace every object of interest concerning the relationship of man to God, if I had time. I can enter into the mysteries; I can enter largely into the eternal worlds; for Jesus said, "In my Father's house are many mansions; if it were not so, I would have told you. I go to prepare a place for you." (John 14:2.) Paul says, "There is one glory of the sun, and another glory of the moon, and another glory of the stars; for one star differeth from another star in glory. So also is the resurrection of the dead." (1 Cor. 15:41.) What have we to console us in relation to the dead? We have reason to have the greatest hope and consolation for our dead of any people on the earth; for we have seen them walk worthily in our midst, and seen them sink asleep in the arms of Jesus; and those who have died in the faith are now in the celestial kingdom of God. And hence is the glory of the sun.

You mourners have occasion to rejoice, speaking of the death of Elder King Follett; for your husband and father is gone to wait until the resurrection of the dead—until the perfection of the remainder; for at the resurrection your friend will rise in perfect felicity and go to celestial glory, while many must wait myriads of years before they can receive the like blessings; and your expectations and hopes are far above what man can conceive; for why has God revealed it to us?

I am authorized to say, by the authority of the Holy Ghost, that you have no occasion to fear; for he [Brother Follett] is gone to the home of the just. Don't mourn, don't weep. I know it by the testimony of the Holy Ghost that is within me; and you may wait for your friends to come forth to meet you in the morn of the celestial world.

Rejoice, O Israel! Your friends who have been murdered for the truth's sake in the persecutions shall triumph gloriously in the celestial world, while their murderers shall welter for ages in torment, even until they shall have paid the uttermost farthing. I say this for the benefit of strangers.

I have a father, brothers, children, and friends who have gone to a world of spirits. They are only absent for a moment. They are in the spirit, and we shall soon meet again. The time will soon arrive when the trumpet shall sound. When we depart, we

16

shall hail our mothers, fathers, friends, and all whom we love, who have fallen asleep in Jesus. There will be no fear of mobs, persecutions, or malicious lawsuits and arrests; but it will be an eternity of felicity.

A question may be asked—"Will mothers have their children in eternity?" Yes! Yes! Mothers, you shall have your children; for they shall have eternal life, for their debt is paid. There is no damnation awaiting them for they are in the spirit. But as the child dies, so shall it rise from the dead, and be for ever living in the learning of God. It will never grow [in the grave]; it will still be the child, in the same precise form [when it rises] as it appeared before it died out of its mother's arms, but possessing all the intelligence of a God. . . .

I will leave this subject here, and make a few remarks on the subject of baptism. The baptism of water, without the baptism of fire and the Holy Ghost attending it, is of no use; they are necessarily and inseparably connected. An individual must be born of water and the spirit in order to get into the kingdom of God. In the German, the text bears me out the same as the revelations which I have given and taught for the past fourteen years on that subject. I have the testimony to put in their teeth. My testimony has been true all the time. You will find it in the declaration of John the Baptist. (Reads from the German.) John says, "I baptize you with water, but when Jesus comes, who has the power (or keys) He shall administer the baptism of fire and the Holy Ghost." Great God! Where is now all the sectarian world? And if this testimony is true, they are all damned as clearly as anathema can do it. I know the text is true. I call upon all you Germans who know that it is true to say, Eye. (Loud shouts of "Aye.")

Alexander Campbell, how are you going to save people with water alone? For John said his baptism was good for nothing without the baptism of Jesus Christ. "Therefore, *not* leaving the principles of the doctrine of Christ, let us go on unto perfection; not laying again the foundation of repentance from dead works, and of faith towards God, of the doctrine of baptism, and of laying on of hands, and of resurrection of the dead, and of eternal judgment. And this will we do, if God permit." (Heb. 6:1–3.)

17

There is one God, one Father, one Jesus, one hope of our calling, one baptism. All these three baptisms only make one. Many talk of baptism not being essential to salvation; but this kind of teaching would lay the foundation of their damnation. I have the truth, and am at the defiance of the world to contradict me, if they can.

I have now preached a little Latin, a little Hebrew, Greek, and German; and I have fulfilled all. I am not so big a fool as many have taken me to be. The Germans know that I read the German correctly.

THE SECOND DEATH

Hear it, all ye ends of the earth—all ye priests, all ye sinners, and all men. Repent! Repent! Obey the gospel. Turn to God; for your religion won't save you, and you will be damned. I do not say how long. There have been remarks made concerning all men being redeemed from hell; but I say that those who sin against the Holy Ghost cannot be forgiven in this world or in the world to come; they shall die the second death. Those who commit the unpardonable sin are doomed to *Gnolom*—to dwell in hell, worlds without end. As they concocted scenes of bloodshed in this world, so they shall rise to that resurrection which is as the lake of fire and brimstone. Some shall rise to the everlasting burnings of God; for God dwells in everlasting burnings and some shall rise to the damnation of their own filthiness, which is as exquisite a torment as the lake of fire and brimstone.

I have intended my remarks for all, both rich and poor, bond and free, great and small. I have no enmity against any man. I love you all; but I hate some of your deeds. I am your best friend, and if persons miss their mark it is their own fault. If I reprove a man, and he hates me, he is a fool; for I love all men, especially these my brethren and sisters.

I rejoice in hearing the testimony of my aged friends. You don't know me; you never knew my heart. No man knows my history. I cannot tell it: I shall never undertake it. I don't blame any one for not believing my history. If I had not experienced what I have, I would not have believed it myself. I never did harm any man since I was born in the world. My voice is always for peace.

I cannot lie down until all my work is finished. I never think any evil, nor do anything to the harm of my fellow-man. When I am called by the trump of the archangel and weighed in the balance, you will all know me then. I add no more. God bless you all. Amen.

The Sermon in the Grove

Joseph Smith

Meeting in the Grove, east of the Temple, June 16, 1844. Prayer by Bishop Newel K. Whitney. Choir sang, "Mortals Awake." President Joseph Smith read the 3rd chapter of Revelation, and took for his text 1st chapter, 6th verse—"And hath made us kings and priests unto God and His Father: to Him be glory and dominion forever and ever. Amen."

[Revelation 1:6] is altogether correct in the [King James] translation. Now, you know that of late some malicious and corrupt men have sprung up and apostatized from the Church of Jesus Christ of Latter-day Saints, and they declare that the Prophet believes in a plurality of Gods, and, lo and behold! we have discovered a very great secret, they cry—"The Prophet says there are many Gods, and this proves that he has fallen."

It has been my intention for a long time to take up this subject and lay it clearly before the people, and show what my faith is in relation to this interesting matter. I have contemplated the saying of Jesus (Luke 17th chapter, 26th verse)—"And as it was in the days of Noah, so shall it be also in the days of the Son of Man." And if it does rain, I'll preach this doctrine, for the truth shall be preached.

PLURALITY OF GODS

I will preach on the plurality of Gods. I have selected this text for that express purpose. I wish to declare I have always and in all congregations when I have preach on the subject of the Deity, it has been the plurality of Gods. It has been preached by the Elders for fifteen years.

I have always declared God to be a distinct personage, Jesus Christ a separate and distinct personage from God the Father, and that the Holy Ghost was a distinct personage and a Spirit: and these three constitute three distinct personages and three Gods. If this is in accordance with the New Testament, lo and behold! we have three Gods anyhow, and they are plural; and who can contradict it?

Our text says, "And hath made us kings and priests unto God and His Father." The Apostles have discovered that there were Gods above, for John says God was the Father of our Lord Jesus Christ. My object was to preach the scriptures, and preach the doctrine they contain, there being a God above, the Father of our Lord Jesus Christ. I am bold to declare I have taught all the strongest doctrines publicly, and always teach stronger doctrines in public than in private.

John was one of the men, and apostles declare they were made kings and priests unto God, the Father of our Lord Jesus Christ. It reads just so in the Revelation, Hence the doctrine of a plurality of Gods is as prominent in the Bible as any other doctrine. It is all over the face of the Bible. It stands beyond the power of controversy. A wayfaring man, though a fool, need not err therein.

Paul says there are Gods many and Lords many. I want to set it forth in a plain and simple manner; but to us there is but one God—that is pertaining to us; and he is in all and through all. But if Joseph Smith says there are Gods many and Lords many, they cry, "Away with him! Crucify him! Crucify him!"

Mankind verily say that the Scriptures are with them. Search the Scriptures, for they testify of things that these apostates would gravely pronounce blasphemy. Paul, if Joseph Smith is a blasphemer, you are. I say there are Gods many and Lords many, but to us only one, and we are to be in subjection to that one, and no man can limit the bounds or the eternal existence of eternal time. Hath he beheld the eternal world, and is he authorized to say that there is only one God? He makes himself a fool if he thinks or says so, and there is an end of his career or progress in knowledge. He cannot obtain all knowledge, for he has sealed up the gate to it.

SCRIPTURAL INTERPRETATION

Some say I do not interpret the Scripture the same as they do. They say it means the heathen's gods. Paul says there are Gods many and Lords many; and that makes a plurality of Gods, in spite of the whims of all men. Without a revelation, I am not going to give them the knowledge of the God of heaven. You know and I testify that Paul had no allusion to the heathen gods. I have it from God, and get over it if you can. I have a witness of the Holy Ghost, and a testimony that Paul had no allusion to the heathen gods in the text. I will show from the Hebrew Bible that I am correct, and the first word shows a plurality of Gods; and I want the apostates and learned men to come here and prove to the contrary, if they can. An unlearned boy must give you a little Hebrew. *Berosheit baurau Eloheim ait aushamayeen vehau auraits,* rendered by King James' translators, "In the beginning God created the heaven and the earth." I want to analyze the word *Berosheit. Rosh,* the head; *Sheit,* a grammatical termination; the *Baith* was not originally put there when the inspired man wrote it, but it has been since added by an old Jew. *Baurau* signifies to bring forth; *Eloheim* is from the word *Eloi,* God, in the singular number; and by adding the word *heim,* it renders it *Gods.* It read first, "In the beginning the head of the Gods brought forth the Gods," or, as others have translated it, "The head of the Gods called the Gods together." I want to show a little learning as well as other fools. . . .

The head God organized the heavens and the earth. I defy all the world to refute me. In the beginning the heads of the Gods organized the heavens and the earth. Now the learned priests and the people rage, and the heathen imagine a vain thing. If we pursue the Hebrew text further, it reads, "The head one of the Gods said, Let us make a man in our own image." I once asked a learned Jew, "If the Hebrew language compels us to render all words ending in *heim* in the plural, why not render the first *Eloheim* plural?" He replied, "That is the rule with few exceptions; but in this case it would ruin the Bible." He acknowledged I was right. I came here to investigate these things precisely as I believe them. Hear and judge for yourselves; and if you go away satisfied, well and good.

In the very beginning the Bible shows there is a plurality of Gods beyond the power of refutation. It is a great subject I am dwelling on. The word *Eloheim* ought to be in the plural all the way through—Gods. The heads of the Gods appointed one God for us; and when you take [that] view of the subject, its sets one free to see all the beauty, holiness and perfection of the Gods. All I want is to get the simple, naked truth, and the whole truth.

Many men say there is one God; the Father, the Son and the Holy Ghost are only one God. I say that is a strange God anyhow—three in one, and one in three! It is a curious organization. "Father, I pray not for the world, but I pray for them which thou hast given me." "Holy Father, keep through Thine own name those whom thou hast given me, that they may be one as we are." All are to be crammed into one God, according to sectarianism. It would make the biggest God in all the world. He would be a wonderfully big God—he would be a giant or a monster. I want to read the text to you myself—"I am agreed with the Father and the Father is agreed with me, and we are agreed as one." The Greek shows that it should be agreed. "Father, I pray for them which Thou hast given me out of the world, and not for those alone, but for them also which shall believe on me through their word, that they all may be agreed, as Thou, Father, are with me, and I with Thee, that they also may be agreed with us," and all come to dwell in unity, and in all the glory and everlasting burnings of the Gods; and then we shall see as we are seen, and be as our God and He as His Father. I want to reason a little on this subject. I learned it by translating the papyrus which is now in my house.

ABRAHAM'S REASONING

I learned a testimony concerning Abraham, and he reasoned concerning the God of heaven. "In order to do that," said he, "suppose we have two facts: that supposes another fact may exist—two men on the earth, one wiser than the other, would logically show that another who is wiser than the wisest may exist. Intelligences exist one above another, so that there is no end to them."

If Abraham reasoned thus—If Jesus Christ was the Son of God, and John discovered that God the Father of Jesus Christ had a Father, you may suppose that He had a Father also. Where was there ever a son without a father? And where was there ever a father without first being a son? Whenever did a tree or anything spring into existence without a progenitor? And everything comes in this way. Paul says that which is earthly is in the likeness of that which is heavenly, Hence if Jesus had a Father, can we not believe that He had a Father also? I despise the idea of being scared to death at such a doctrine, for the Bible is full of it.

I want you to pay particular attention to what I am saying. Jesus said that the Father wrought precisely in the same way as His Father had done before Him. As the Father had done before? He laid down His life, and took it up the same as His Father had done before. He did as He was sent, to lay down His life and take it up again; and then was committed unto Him the keys. I know it is good reasoning.

THE CHURCH BEING PURGED

I have reason to think that the Church is being purged. I saw Satan fall from heaven, and the way they ran was a caution. All these are wonders and marvels in our eyes in these last days. So long as men are under the law of God, they have no fears—they do not scare themselves.

I want to stick to my text, to show that when men open their lips against these truths they do not injure me, but injure themselves. To the law and to the testimony, for these principles are poured out all over the Scriptures. When things that are of the greatest importance are passed over by the weak-minded men without even a thought, I want to see truth in all its bearings and hug it to my bosom. I believe all that God ever revealed, and I never hear of a man being damned for believing too much; but they are damned for unbelief.

They found fault with Jesus Christ because He said He was the Son of God, and made Himself equal with God. They say of me, like they did of the Apostles of old, that I must be put down. What did Jesus say? "Is it not written in your law, I said, Ye are Gods? If He called them Gods unto whom the word of God came, and the Scriptures cannot be broken, say ye of Him whom the Father hath sanctified and sent into the world, Thou blasphemest; because I said I am the Son of God?" It was through Him that they drank of the spiritual rock. Of course He would take the honor to Himself. Jesus, if they were called Gods unto whom the word of God came, why should it be thought blasphemy that I should say I am the Son of God?

ETERNAL GLORIES

Go and read the vision in the Book of Covenants. There is clearly illustrated glory upon glory—one glory of the sun, another glory of the moon, and a glory of the stars; and as one star differeth from another star in glory, even so do they of the telestial world differ in glory, and every man who reigns in celestial glory is a God to his dominions. By the apostates admitting the testimony of the Doctrine and Covenants they damn themselves. Paul, what do you say? They impeached Paul and all went and left him. Paul had seven churches, and they drove him off from among them; and yet they cannot do it by me. I rejoice in that. My testimony is good.

Paul says, "There is one glory of the sun, and another glory of the moon, and another glory of the stars; for one star differeth from another star in glory. So also is the resurrection of the dead." They who obtain a glorious resurrection from the dead, are exalted far above principalities, powers, thrones, dominions and angels, and are expressly declared to be heirs of God and joint heirs with Jesus Christ, all having eternal power.

These Scriptures are a mixture of very strange doctrines to the Christian world, who are blindly led by the blind. I will refer to another Scripture. "Now," says God, when He visited Moses in the bush (Moses was a stammering sort of a boy like me), God said, "Thou shalt be a God unto the children of Israel." God said, "Thou shalt be a God unto Aaron, and he shall be thy spokesman." I believe those Gods that God reveals as Gods to be sons of God, and all can cry, "Abba, Father!" Sons of God who exalt themselves to be Gods, even from before the foundation of the world, and are the only Gods I have a reverence for.

John said he was a king. "And from Jesus Christ, who is the faithful witness, and the first begotten of the dead, and the Prince of the kings of the earth. Unto Him that loved us, and washed us from our sins in His own blood, and hath made us kings and priests unto God, and His Father; to him be glory and dominion forever and ever, Amen." Oh, Thou God who art King of kings and Lord of lords, the sectarian world, by their actions, declare, "We cannot believe Thee."

The old Catholic church traditions are worth more than all you have said. Here is a principle of logic that most men have no more sense than to adopt. I will illustrate it by an old apple tree. Here jumps off a branch and says, I am the true tree, and you are corrupt. If the whole tree is corrupt, are not its branches corrupt? If the Catholic religion is a false religion, how can any true religion come out of it? If the Catholic church is bad, how can any good thing come out of it? The character of the old churches have always been slandered by all apostates since the world began.

THE LORD WILL NOT ACKNOWLEDGE TRAITORS

I testify again, as the Lord lives, God never will acknowledge any traitors or apostates. Any man who will betray the Catholics will betray you; and if he will betray me, he will betray you. All men are liars who say they are of the true Church without the revelations of Jesus Christ and the Priesthood of Melchizedek, which is after the order of the Son of God.

It is in the order of heavenly things that God should always send a new dispensation into the world when men have apostatized from the truth and lost the priesthood, but when men come out and build upon other men's foundations, they do it on their own responsibility, without authority from God; and when the floods come and the winds blow, their foundations will be found to be sand, and their whole fabric will crumble to dust.

Did I build on any other man's foundation? I have got all the truth which the Christian world possessed, and an independent revelation in the bargain, and God will bear me off triumphant. I will drop this subject. I wish I could speak for three or four hours; but it is not expedient on account of the rain; I would still go on, and show you proof upon proofs; all the Bible is equal in support of this doctrine, one part as another.

The Wentworth Letter

Joseph Smith

March 1, 1842.—At the request of Mr. John Wentworth, Editor and Proprietor of the Chicago Democrat. I have written the following sketch of the rise, progress, persecution, and faith of the Latter-day Saints, of which I have the honor, under God, of being the founder. Mr. Wentworth says that he wishes to furnish Mr. Bastow, a friend of his, who is writing the history of New Hampshire, with this document. As Mr. Bastow has taken the proper steps to obtain correct information, all that I shall ask at his hands, is, that he publish the account entire, ungarnished, and without misrepresentation.

I was born in the town of Sharon, Windsor County, Vermont, on the 23rd of December, A.D. 1805. When ten years old, my parents removed to Palmyra, New York, where we resided about four years, and from thence we removed to the town of Manchester. My father was a farmer and taught me the art of husbandry. When about fourteen years of age, I began to reflect upon the importance of being prepared for a future state, and upon inquiring [about] the plan of salvation, I found that there was a great clash in religious sentiment; if I went to one society they referred me to one plan, and another to another; each one pointing to his own particular creed as the summum bonum of perfection. Considering that all could not be right, and that God could not be the author of so much confusion, I determined to investigate the subject more fully, believing that if God had a Church it would not be split up into factions, and that if He taught one society to worship one way, and administer in one set of ordinances, He would not teach another, principles which were diametrically opposed.

Believing the word of God, I had confidence in the declaration of James—"If any of you lack wisdom, let him ask of God, that giveth to all men liberally, and upbraideth not; and it shall be given him." I retired to a secret place in a grove, and began to call upon the Lord; while fervently engaged in supplication, my mind was taken away from the objects with which I was surrounded, and I was enwrapped in a heavenly vision, and saw two glorious personages, who exactly resembled each other in features and likeness, surrounded with a brilliant light which eclipsed the sun at noon day. They told me that all religious denominations were believing in incorrect doctrines, and that none of them was acknowledged of God as His Church and kingdom: and I was expressly commanded "to go not after them," at the same time receiving a promise that the fullness of the Gospel should at some future time be made known unto me.

On the evening on the 21st of September, A.D. 1823, while I was praying unto God, and endeavoring to exercise faith in the precious promises of Scripture, on a sudden a light like that of day, only of a far purer and more glorious appearance and brightness, burst into the room, indeed the first sight was as though the house was filled with consuming fire; the appearance produced a shock that affected the whole body; in a moment a personage stood before me surrounded with a glory yet greater than that with which I was already surrounded. This messenger proclaimed himself to be an angel of God, sent to bring the joyful tidings that the covenant which God made with ancient Israel was at hand to be fulfilled, that the preparatory work for the second coming of the Messiah was speedily to commence; that the time was at hand for the Gospel in all its fullness to be preached in power, unto all nations that a people might be prepared for the Millennial reign. I was informed that I was chosen to be an instrument in the hands of God to bring about some of His purposes in this glorious dispensation.

I was also informed concerning the aboriginal inhabitants of this country and shown who they were, and from whence they came; a brief sketch of their origin, progress, civilization, laws, governments, of their righteousness and iniquity, and the blessings of God being finally withdrawn from them as a people, was made known unto me; I was also told where were deposited some plates on which were engraven an abridgment of the records of the ancient Prophets that had existed on this continent. The angel appeared to me three times the same night and unfolded the same things. After having received many visits from the angels of God unfolding the majesty and glory of the events that should transpire in the last days, on the morning of the 22nd of September, A.D. 1827, the angel of the Lord delivered the records into my hands.

These records were engraven on plates which had the appearance of gold, each plate was six inches wide and eight inches long, and not quite so thick as common tin. They were filled with engravings, in Egyptian characters, and bound together in a volume as the leaves of a book, with three rings running through the whole. The volume was something near six inches in thickness, a part of which was sealed. The characters on the unsealed part were small, and beautifully engraved. The whole book exhibited many marks of antiquity in its construction, and much skill in the art of engraving. With the records was found a curious instrument, which the ancients called "Urim and Thummim," which consisted of two transparent stones set in the rims of a bow fastened to a breast plate. Through the medium of the Urim and Thummim I translated the record by the gift and power of God.

In this important and interesting book the history of ancient America is unfolded, from its first settlement by a colony that came from the Tower of Babel, at the confusion of languages to the beginning of the fifth century of the Christian Era. We are informed by these records that America in ancient times has been inhabited by two distinct races of people. The first were called Jaredites, and came directly from the Tower of Babel. The second race came directly from the city of Jerusalem, about six hundred years before Christ. They were principally Israelites, of the descendants of Joseph. The Jaredites were destroyed about the time that the Israelites came from Jerusalem, who succeeded them in the inheritance of the country. The principal nation of the second race fell in battle towards the close of the fourth century. The remnant are the Indians that now inhabit this country.

31

This book also tells us that our Savior made His appearance unto this continent after His resurrection; that He planted the Gospel here in all its fulness, and richness, and power, and blessing; that they had Apostles, Prophets, Pastors, Teachers, and Evangelists; the same order, the same priesthood, the same ordinances, gifts, powers, and blessings, as were enjoyed on the eastern continent, that the people were cut off in consequence of their transgressions, that the last of their prophets who existed among them was commanded to write an abridgment of their prophecies, history, &c, and to hide it up in the earth, and that it should come forth and be united with the Bible for the accomplishment of the purposes of God in the last days. For a more particular account I would refer to the Book of Mormon, which can be purchased at Nauvoo, or from any of our Traveling Elders.

As soon as the news of this discovery was made known, false reports, misrepresentation and slander flew, as on the wings of the wind, in every direction; the house was frequently beset by mobs and evil designing people. Several times I was shot at, and very narrowly escaped, and every device was made use of to get the plates away from me; but the power and blessing of God attended me, and several began to believe my testimony.

On the 6th of April, 1830, the "Church of Jesus Christ of Latterday Saints" was first organized in the town of Fayette, Seneca county, state of New York. Some few were called and ordained by the Spirit of revelation and prophecy, and began to preach as the Spirit gave them utterance, and though weak, yet were they strengthened by the power of God, and many were brought to repentance, were immersed in the water, and were filled with the Holy Ghost by the laying on of hands. They saw visions and prophesied, devils were cast out, and the sick healed by the laying on of hands. From that time the work rolled forth with astonishing rapidity, and churches were formed in the states of New York, Pennsylvania, Ohio, Indiana, Illinois, and Missouri; in the last named state a considerable settlement was formed in Jackson county: numbers joined the Church and we were increasing rapidly; we made large purchases of land, our farms teemed with plenty, and peace and happiness were enjoyed in our domestic circle, and throughout our neighborhood; but as we could not associate with our neighbors (who were, many of them, of the basest of men, and had fled from the face of civilized society, to the frontier country to escape the hand of justice,) in their midnight revels, their Sabbath breaking, horse racing and gambling; they commenced at first to ridicule, then to persecute, and finally an organized mob assembled and burned our houses, tarred and feathered and whipped many of our brethren, and finally, contrary to law, justice and humanity, drove them from their habitations; who, houseless and homeless, had to wander on the bleak prairies till the children left the tracks of their blood on the prairie. This took place in the month of November, and they had no other covering but the canopy of heaven, in this inclement season of the year; this proceeding was winked at by the government, and although we had warrantee deeds for our land, and had violated no law, we could obtain no redress.

There were many sick, who were thus inhumanly driven from their houses, and had to endure all this abuse and to seek homes where they could be found. The result was, that a great many of them being deprived of the comforts of life, and the necessary attendances, died; many children were left orphans, wives, widows and husbands, widowers; our farms were taken possession of by the mob, many thousands of cattle, sheep, horses and hogs were taken, and our household goods, store goods, and printing press and type were broken, taken, or otherwise destroyed.

Many of our brethren removed to Clay county, where they continued until 1836, three years; there was no violence offered, but there were threatenings of violence. But in the summer of 1836 these threatenings began to assume a more serious form, from threats, public meetings were called, resolutions were passed, vengeance and destruction were threatened, and affairs again assumed a fearful attitude, Jackson county was a sufficient precedent, and as the authorities in that county did not interfere they boasted that they would not in this; which on application to the authorities we found to be too true, and after much privation and loss of property, we were again driven from our homes.

We next settled in Caldwell and Daviess counties, where we made large and extensive settlements, thinking to free ourselves from the power of oppression, by settling in new counties, with very few inhabitants in them; but here we were not allowed to live in peace, but in 1838 we were again attacked by mobs, an exterminating order was issued by Governor Boggs, and under the sanction of law, an organized banditti ranged through the country, robbed us of our cattle, sheep, hogs, &c., many of our people were murdered in cold blood, the chastity of our women was violated, and we were forced to sign away our property at the point of the sword; and after enduring every indignity that could be heaped upon us by an inhuman, ungodly band of marauders, from twelve to fifteen thousand souls, men, women, and children were driven from their own firesides, and from lands to which they had warrantee deeds, houseless, friendless, and homeless (in the depths of winter) to wander as exiles on the earth, or to seek an asylum in a more genial clime, and among a less barbarous people. Many sickened and died in consequence of the cold and hardships they had to endure; many wives were left widows, and children, orphans, and destitute. It would take more time than is allotted me here to describe the injustice, the wrongs, the murders the bloodshed, the theft, misery and woe that have been caused by the barbarous, inhuman, and lawless proceedings of the state of Missouri.

In the situation before alluded to, we arrived in the state of Illinois in 1839, where we found a hospitable people and a friendly home: a people who were willing to be governed by the principles of law and humanity. We have commenced to build a city called "Nauvoo," in Hancock county. We number from six to eight thousand here, besides vast numbers in the county around, and in almost every county of the state. We have a city charter granted us, and charter for a Legion, the troops of which now number 1,500. We have also a charter for a University, for an Agricultural and Manufacturing Society, have our own laws and administrators, and possess all the privileges that other free and enlightened citizens enjoy.

Persecution has not stopped the progress of truth, but has only added fuel to the flame, it has spread with increasing rapidity. Proud of the cause which they have espoused, and conscious of our innocence, and of the truth of their system, 'midst calumny and reproach, have the Elders of this Church gone forth, and planted the Gospel in almost every state in the Union; it has penetrated our cities, it has spread over our villages, and has caused thousands of our intelligent, noble, and patriotic citizens to obey its divine mandates, and be governed by its sacred truths. It has also spread into England, Ireland, Scotland, and Wales, where, in the year 1840, a few of our missionaries were sent, and over five thousand joined the Standard of Truth; there are numbers now joining in every land.

Our missionaries are going forth to different nations, and in Germany, Palestine, New Holland, Australia, the East Indies, and other places, the Standard of Truth has been erected; no unhallowed hand can stop the work from progressing; persecutions may rage, mobs may combine, armies may assemble, calumny may defame, but the truth of God will go forth boldly, nobly, and independent, till it has penetrated every continent, visited every clime, swept every country, and sounded in every ear, till the purposes of God shall be accomplished, and the Great Jehovah shall say the work is done.

We believe in God the eternal Father, and in His Son Jesus Christ, and in the Holy Ghost.

We believe that men will be punished according to their own sins and not for Adam's transgression.

We believe that through the atonement of Christ all mankind may be saved by obedience to the laws and ordinances of the Gospel.

We believe that the first principles and ordinances of the Gospel are: (1) Faith in the Lord Jesus Christ; (2) Repentance; (3) Baptism by immersion for the remission of sins; (4) Laying on of hands for the gift of the Holy Ghost.

We believe that a man must be called of God by prophecy and by the laying on hands, by those who are in authority, to preach the Gospel and administer in the ordinances thereof.

We believe in the same organization that existed in the primitive Church, viz: apostles, prophets, pastors, teachers, evangelists, etc.

We believe in the gift of tongues, prophecy, revelation, visions, healing, interpretation of tongues, etc.

We believe the Bible to be the word of God, as far as it is translated correctly; we also believe the Book of Mormon to be the word of God.

We believe all that God has revealed, all that He does now reveal, and we believe that He will yet reveal many great and important things pertaining to the kingdom of God.

We believe in the literal gathering of Israel and in the restoration of the Ten Tribes; that Zion will be built upon this [the American] continent; that Christ will reign personally upon the earth; and that the earth will be renewed and receive its paradisiacal glory.

We claim the privilege of worshiping Almighty God according to the dictates of our own conscience, and allow all men the same privilege, let them worship how, where, or what they may.

We believe in being subject to kings, presidents, rulers and magistrates, in obeying, honoring, and sustaining the law.

We believe in being honest, true, chaste, benevolent, virtuous, and in doing good to all men; indeed we may say that we follow the admonition of Paul, "We believe all things, we hope all things, we have endured many things, and hope to be able to endure all things. If there is anything virtuous, lovely, or of good report, or praiseworthy, we seek after these things.

Respectfully, &c., JOSEPH SMITH.

The Father and the Son

A Doctrinal Exposition by the First Presidency and the Twelve

The scriptures plainly and repeatedly affirm that God is the Creator of the earth and the heavens and all things that in them are. In the sense so expressed the Creator is an Organizer. God created the earth as an organized sphere; but He certainly did not create, in the sense of bringing into primal existence, the ultimate elements of the materials of which the earth consists, for "the elements are eternal" (D&C 93:33).

So also life is eternal, and not created; but life, or the vital force, may be infused into organized matter, though the details of the process have not been revealed unto man. For illustrative instances see Genesis 2:7; Moses 3:7; and Abraham 5:7. Each of these scriptures states that God breathed into the body of man the breath of life. See further Moses 3:19, for the statement that God breathed the breath of life into the bodies of the beasts and birds. God showed unto Abraham "the intelligences that were organized before the world was"; and by "intelligences" we are to understand personal "spirits" (Abraham 3:22, 23); nevertheless, we are expressly told that "Intelligence" that is, "the light of truth was not created or made, neither indeed can be" (D&C 93:29).

The term "Father" as applied to Deity occurs in sacred writ with plainly different meanings. Each of the four significations specified in the following treatment should be carefully segregated.

1. "FATHER" AS LITERAL PARENT

Scriptures embodying the ordinary signification—literally that of Parent—are too numerous and specific to require citation. The purport of these scriptures is to the effect that God the Eternal Father, whom we designate by the exalted name-title "Elohim," is the literal Parent of our Lord and Savior Jesus Christ, and of the spirits of the human race. Elohim is the Father in every sense in which Jesus Christ is so designated, and distinctively He is the Father of spirits. Thus we read in the Epistle to the Hebrews: "Furthermore we have had fathers of our flesh which corrected us, and we gave them reverence; shall we not much rather be in subjection unto the Father of spirits, and live?" (Hebrews 12:9). In view of this fact we are taught by Jesus Christ to pray: "Our Father which art in heaven, Hallowed be thy name."

Jesus Christ applies to Himself both titles, "Son" and "Father." Indeed, He specifically said to the brother of Jared: "Behold, I am Jesus Christ. I am the Father and the Son" (Ether 3:14). Jesus Christ is the Son of Elohim both as spiritual and bodily offspring; that is to say, Elohim is literally the Father of the spirit of Jesus Christ and also of the body in which Jesus Christ performed His mission in the flesh, and which body died on the cross and was afterward taken up by the process of resurrection, and is now the immortalized tabernacle of the eternal spirit of our Lord and Savior. No extended explanation of the title "Son of God" as applied to Jesus Christ appears necessary.

2. "FATHER" AS CREATOR

A second scriptural meaning of "Father" is that of Creator, e. g. in passages referring to any one of the Godhead as "The Father of the heavens and of the earth and all things that in them are" (Ether 4:7; see also Alma 11:38, 39 and Mosiah 15:4).

God is not the Father of the earth as one of the worlds in space, nor of the heavenly bodies in whole or in part, nor of the inanimate objects and the plants and the animals upon the earth, in the literal sense in which He is the Father of the spirits of mankind. Therefore, scriptures that refer to God in any way as the Father of the heavens and the earth are to be understood as signifying that God is the Maker, the Organizer, the Creator of the heavens and the earth.

With this meaning, as the context shows in every case, Jehovah, who is Jesus Christ the Son of Elohim, is called "the Father," and even "the very eternal Father of heaven and of earth" (see passages before cited, and also Mosiah 16:15). With analogous meaning Jesus Christ is called "The Everlasting Father" (Isaiah 9:6; compare 2 Nephi 19:6). The descriptive titles "Everlasting" and "Eternal" in the foregoing texts are synonymous.

That Jesus Christ, whom we also know as Jehovah, was the executive of the Father, Elohim, in the work of creation is set forth in the book "Jesus the Christ" Chapter 4. Jesus Christ, being the Creator, is consistently called the Father of heaven and earth in the sense explained above; and since His creations are of eternal quality He is very properly called the Eternal Father of heaven and earth.

3. JESUS CHRIST THE "FATHER" OF THOSE WHO ABIDE IN HIS GOSPEL

A third sense in which Jesus Christ is regarded as the "Father" has reference to the relationship between Him and those who accept His Gospel and thereby become heirs of eternal life. Following are a few of the scriptures illustrating this meaning.

In the fervent prayer offered just prior to His entrance into Gethsemane, Jesus Christ supplicated His Father in behalf of those whom the Father had given unto Him, specifically the apostles, and, more generally, all who would accept and abide in the Gospel through the ministry of the apostles. Read in our Lord's own words the solemn affirmation that those for whom He particularly prayed were His own, and that His Father had given them unto Him: "I have manifested thy name unto the men which thou gavest me out of the world: thine they were, and thou gavest them me; and they have kept thy word. Now they have known that all things whatsoever thou hast given me are of thee. For I have given unto them the words which thou gavest me; and they have received them, and have known surely that I came out from thee, and they have believed that thou didst send me. I pray for them: I pray not for the world, but for them which thou hast given me; for they are thine. And all mine are thine, and thine are mine; and I am glorified in them. And now I am no more in the world, but these are in the world, and I come to thee. Holy Father, keep through thine own name those whom thou hast given me, that they may be one as we are. While I was with them in the world, I kept them in thy name: those that thou gavest me I have kept, and none of them is lost, but the son of perdition; that the scripture might be fulfilled" (John 17:6–12).

And further: "Neither pray I for these alone, but for them also which shall believe on me through their word; That they all may be one; as thou, Father, art in me, and I in thee, that they also may be one in us: that the world may believe that thou hast sent me. And the glory which thou gavest me I have given them; that they may be one, even as we are one: I in them, and thou in me, that they may be made perfect in one; and that the world may know that thou hast sent me, and hast loved them, as thou hast loved me. Father, I will that they also, whom thou hast given me, be with me where I am; that they may behold my glory, which thou hast given me: for thou lovedst me before the foundation of the world" (John 17:20–24).

To His faithful servants in the present dispensation the Lord has said: "Fear not, little children; for you are mine, and I have overcome the world, and you are of them that my Father hath given me" (D&C 50:41).

Salvation is attainable only through compliance with the laws and ordinances of the Gospel; and all who are thus saved become sons and daughters unto God in a distinctive sense. In a revelation given through Joseph the Prophet to Emma Smith the Lord Jesus addressed the woman as "My daughter," and said: "for verily I say unto you, all those who receive my gospel are sons and daughters in my kingdom" (D&C 25:1). In many instances the Lord has addressed men as His sons (e.g. D&C 9:1; 34:3; 121:7).

That by obedience to the Gospel men may become sons of God, both as sons of Jesus Christ, and, through Him, as sons of His Father, is set forth in many revelations given in the current dispensation. Thus we read in an utterance of the Lord Jesus Christ to Hyrum Smith in 1829: "Behold, I am Jesus Christ, the Son of God. I am the life and the light of the world. I am the same who came unto my own and my own received me not; but verily, verily, I say unto you, that as many as receive me, to them will I give power to become the sons of God, even to them that believe on my name. Amen." (D&C 11:28–30). To Orson Pratt the Lord spoke through Joseph the Seer, in 1830: "My son Orson, hearken and hear and behold what I, the Lord God, shall say unto you, even Jesus Christ your Redeemer; The light and the life of the world; a light which shineth in darkness and the darkness comprehendeth it not; Who so loved the world that he gave his own life, that as many as would believe might come the sons of God: wherefore you are my son" (D&C 34:1–3). In 1830 the Lord thus addressed Joseph Smith and Sidney Rigdon: "Listen to the voice of the Lord your God, even Alpha and Omega, the beginning and the end, whose course is one eternal round, the same today as yesterday, and for ever. I am Jesus Christ, the Son of God, who was crucified for the sins of the world, even as many as will believe on my name, that they may become the sons of God, even one in me as I am in the Father, as the Father is one in me, that we may be one" (D&C 35:1–2). Consider also the following given in 1831: "Hearken and listen to the voice of him who is from all eternity to all eternity, the Great I AM, even Jesus Christ, the light and the life of the world; a light which shineth in darkness and the darkness comprehendeth it not: the same which came in the meridian of time unto my own, and my own received me not; but to as many as received me, gave I power to become my sons, and even so will I give unto as many as will receive me, power to become my sons" (D&C 39:1–4). In a revelation given through Joseph Smith in March, 1831 we read: "For verily I say unto you that I am Alpha and Omega, the beginning and the end, the light and the life of the world—a light that shineth in darkness and the darkness comprehendeth it not. I came unto my own, and my own received me not; but unto as many as received me, gave I power to do many miracles, and to become the sons of God, and even unto them that believed on my name gave I power to obtain eternal life" (D&C 45:7–8).

A forceful exposition of this relationship between Jesus Christ as the Father and those who comply with the requirements of the Gospel as His children was given by Abinadi, centuries before our Lord's birth in the flesh: "And now I say unto you. Who shall declare his generation? Behold, I say unto you, that when his soul has been made an offering for sin, he shall see his seed. And now what say ye? And who shall be his seed? Behold I say unto you, that whosoever has heard the words of the prophets, yea, all the holy prophets who have prophesied concerning the coming of the Lord; I say unto you, that all those who have hearkened unto their words, and believed that the Lord would redeem his people, and have looked forward to that day for a remission of their sins; I say unto you, that these are his seed, or they are the heirs of the kingdom of God: For these are they whose sins he has borne; these are they for whom he has died, to redeem them from their transgressions. And now, are they not his seed? Yea, and are not the prophets, every one that has opened his mouth to prophesy, that has not fallen into transgression; I mean all the holy prophets ever since the world began? I say unto you that they are his seed" (Mosiah 15:10–13).

In tragic contrast with the blessed state of those who become children of God through obedience to the Gospel of Jesus Christ is that of the unregenerate, who are specifically called the children of the devil. Note the words of Christ, while in the flesh, to certain wicked Jews who boasted of their Abrahamic lineage: "If ye were Abraham's children, ye would do the works of Abraham.

Ye do the deeds of your father. If God were your Father, ye would love me. Ye are of your father the devil, and the lusts of your father ye will do" (John 8:39, 41, 42, 44). Thus Satan is designated as the father of the wicked, though we cannot assume any personal relationship of parent and children as existing between him and them. A combined illustration showing that the righteous are the children of God and the wicked the children of the devil appears in the parable of the Tares: "The good seed are the children of the kingdom; but the tares are the children of the wicked one" (Matt. 13:38).

Men may become children of Jesus Christ by being born anew—born of God, as the inspired word states: "He that committeth sin is of the devil; for the devil sinneth from the beginning. For this purpose the Son of God was manifested, that he might destroy the works of the devil. Whosoever is born of God doth not commit sin; for his seed remaineth in him: and he cannot sin, because he is born of God. In this the children of God are manifest, and the children of the devil: Whosoever doeth not righteousness is not of God, neither he that loveth not his brother" (I John 3:8–10).

Those who have been born unto God through obedience to the Gospel may by valiant devotion to righteousness obtain exaltation and even reach the status of Godhood. Of such we read: "Wherefore, as it is written, they are Gods, even the sons of God" (D&C 76:58; compare 132:20, and contrast paragraph 17 in same section; see also paragraph 37). Yet, though they be Gods they are still subject to Jesus Christ as their Father in this exalted relationship; and so we read in the paragraph following the above quotation: "and they are Christ's and Christ is God's" (76:59).

By the new birth—that of water and the Spirit—mankind may become children of Jesus Christ, being through the means by Him provided "begotten sons and daughters unto God" (D&C 76:2). This solemn truth is further emphasized in the words of the Lord Jesus Christ given through Joseph Smith in 1833: "And now, verily I say unto you, I was in the beginning with the Father, and am the firstborn; And all those who are begotten through me are partakers of the glory of the same, and are the church of the firstborn" (D&C 93:21, 22). For such figurative use of the term "begotten" in application to those who are born unto God see Paul's explanation: "for in Christ Jesus I have begotten you through the gospel" (I Cor. 4:15). An analogous instance of sonship attained by righteous service is found in the revelation relating to the order and functions of Priesthood, given in 1832: "For whoso is faithful unto the obtaining these two Priesthoods of which I have spoken, and the magnifying their calling, are sanctified by the Spirit unto the renewing of their bodies: They become the sons of Moses and of Aaron and the seed of Abraham, and the church and kingdom, and the elect of God" (D&C 84:33, 34).

If it be proper to speak of those who accept and abide in the Gospel as Christ's sons and daughters—and upon this matter the scriptures are explicit and cannot be gainsaid nor denied—it is consistently proper to speak of Jesus Christ as the Father of the righteous, they having become His children and He having been made their Father through the second birth—the baptismal regeneration.

4. JESUS CHRIST THE "FATHER" BY DIVINE INVESTITURE OF AUTHORITY

A fourth reason for applying the title "Father" to Jesus Christ is found in the fact that in all His dealings with the human family Jesus the Son has represented and yet represents Elohim His Father in power and authority. This is true of Christ in His pre-existent, antemortal, or unembodied state, in the which He was known as Jehovah; also during His embodiment in the flesh; and during His labors as a disembodied spirit in the realm of the dead; and since that period in His resurrected state. To the Jews He said: "I and my Father are one" (John 10:30; see also 17:11, 22); yet He declared "My Father is greater than I" (John 14:28); and further, "I am come in my Father's name" (John 5:43; see also 10:25). The same truth was declared by Christ Himself to the Nephites (see 3 Nephi 20:35 and 28:10), and has been reaffirmed by revelation in the present dispensation (Doc. & Gov. 50:43). Thus the Father placed His name upon the Son; and Jesus Christ spoke and ministered in and through the Father's name; and so far as power, authority and Godship are concerned His words and acts were and are those of the Father.

We read, by way of analogy, that God placed His name upon or in the Angel who was assigned to special ministry unto the people of Israel during the exodus. Of that Angel the Lord said: "Beware of him, and obey his voice, provoke him not; for he will not pardon your transgressions: for my name is in him" (Exodus 23:21).

The ancient apostle, John, was visited by an angel who ministered and spoke in the name of Jesus Christ. As we read: "The Revelation of Jesus Christ, which God gave unto him, to shew unto his servants things which must shortly come to pass; and he sent and signified it by his angel unto his servant John" (Revelation 1:1). John was about to worship the angelic being who spoke in the name of the Lord Jesus Christ, but was forbidden: "And I John saw these things, and heard them. And when I had heard and seen, I fell down to worship before the feet of the angel which showed me these things. Then saith he unto me, See thou do it not: for I am thy fellow-servant, and of thy brethren the prophets, and of them which keep the sayings of this book: worship God" (Rev. 22:8, 9). And then the angel continued to speak as though he were the Lord Himself: "And, behold, I come quickly; and my reward is with me, to give every man according as his work shall be. I am Alpha and Omega, the beginning and the end, the first and the last" (verses 12, 13). The resurrected Lord, Jesus Christ, who had been exalted to the right hand of God His Father, had placed His name upon the angel sent to John, and the angel spoke in the first person, saying "I come quickly," "I am Alpha and Omega," though he meant that Jesus Christ would come, and that Jesus Christ was Alpha and Omega.

None of these considerations, however, can change in the least degree the solemn fact of the literal relationship of Father and Son between Elohim and Jesus Christ. Among the spirit children of Elohim the firstborn was and is Jehovah or Jesus Christ to whom all others are juniors. Following are affirmative scriptures bearing upon this great truth. Paul, writing to the Colossians, says of Jesus Christ: "Who is the image of the invisible God, the firstborn of every creature: For by him were all things created, that are in heaven, and that are in earth, visible and invisible, whether they be thrones, or dominions, or principalities, or powers; all things were created by him, and for him: And he is before all things, and by him all things consist. And he is the head of the body, the church: who is the beginning, the firstborn from the dead; that in all things he might have the preeminence. For it pleased the Father that in him should all fullness dwell" (Colossians 1:15–19). From this scripture we learn that Jesus Christ was "the firstborn of every creature" and it is evident that the seniority here expressed must be with respect to antemortal existence, for Christ was not the senior of all mortals in the flesh. He is further designated as "the firstborn from the dead" this having reference to Him as the first to be resurrected from the dead, or as elsewhere written "the first fruits of them that slept" (I Corinthians 15:20, see also verse 23); and "the first begotten of the dead" (Revelation 1:5; compare Acts 26:23). The writer of the Epistle to the Hebrews affirms the status of Jesus Christ as the firstborn of the spirit children of His Father, and extols the preeminence of the Christ when tabernacled in flesh: "And again, when he bringeth in the first begotten into the world, he saith, And let all the angels of God worship him" (Hebrews 1:6; read the preceding verses). That the spirits who were juniors to Christ were predestined to be born in the image of their Elder Brother is thus attested by Paul: "And we know that all things work together for good to them that love God, to them who are the called according to his purpose. For whom he did foreknow, he also did predestinate to be conformed to the image of his Son, that he might be the firstborn among many brethren" (Romans 8:28, 29). John the Revelator was commanded to write to the head of the Laodicean church, as the words of the Lord Jesus Christ: "These things saith the Amen, the faithful and true witness, the beginning of the creation of God" (Revelation 3:14). In the course of a revelation given through Joseph Smith in May, 1833, the Lord Jesus Christ said as before cited: "And now, verily I say unto you, I was in the beginning with the Father, and am the firstborn" (D&C 93:21). A later verse makes plain the fact that human beings generally were similarly existent in spirit state prior to their embodiment in the flesh: "Ye were also in the beginning with the Father; that which is Spirit, even the Spirit of truth" (verse 23).

There is no impropriety, therefore, in speaking of Jesus Christ as the Elder Brother of the rest of human kind. That He is by spiritual birth Brother to the rest of us is indicated in Hebrews:

46

"Wherefore in all things it behoved him to be made like unto his brethren, that he might be a merciful and faithful high priest in things pertaining to God, to make reconciliation for the sins of the people" (Hebrews 2:17). Let it not be forgotten, however, that He is essentially greater than any and all others, by reason (1) of His seniority as the oldest or firstborn; (2) of His unique status in the flesh as the offspring of a mortal mother and of an immortal, or resurrected and glorified, Father; (3) of His selection and foreordination as the one and only Redeemer and Savior of the race; and (4) of His transcendent sinlessness.

Jesus Christ is not the Father of the spirits who have taken or yet shall take bodies upon this earth, for He is one of them. He is The Son, as they are sons or daughters of Elohim. So far as the stages of eternal progression and attainment have been made known through divine revelation, we are to understand that only resurrected and glorified beings can become parents of spirit offspring. Only such exalted souls have reached maturity in the appointed course of eternal life; and the spirits born to them in the eternal worlds will pass in due sequence through the several stages or estates by which the glorified parents have attained exaltation.

The Origin of Man

The First Presidency of the Church

"God created man in his own image."

Inquiries arise from time to time respecting the attitude of the Church of Jesus Christ of Latter-day Saints upon questions which, though not vital from a doctrinal standpoint, are closely connected with the fundamental principles of salvation. The latest inquiry of this kind that has reached us is in relation to the origin of man. It is believed that a statement of the position held by the Church upon this important subject will be timely and productive of good.

In presenting the statement that follows we are not conscious of putting forth anything essentially new; neither is it our desire so to do. Truth is what we wish to present, and truth—eternal truth—is fundamentally old. A restatement of the original attitude of the Church relative to this matter is all that will be attempted here. To tell the truth as God has revealed it, and commend it to the acceptance of those who need to conform their opinions thereto, is the sole purpose of this presentation.

"God created man in his own image, in the image of God created he him; male and female created he them." In these plain and pointed words the inspired author of the book of Genesis made known to the world the truth concerning the origin of the human family. Moses, the prophet-historian, "learned," as we are told, "in all the wisdom of the Egyptians," when making this important announcement, was not voicing a mere opinion, a theory derived from his researches into the occult lore of that ancient people. He was speaking as the mouthpiece of God, and his solemn declaration was for all time and for all people. No subsequent revelator of the truth has contradicted the great leader and lawgiver of Israel. All who have since spoken by divine authority upon this theme have confirmed his simple and sublime proclamation. Nor could it be otherwise. Truth has but one source, and all revelations from heaven are harmonious with each other. The omnipotent Creator, the maker of heaven and earth—had shown unto Moses everything pertaining to this planet, including the facts relating to man's origin, and the authoritative pronouncement of that mighty prophet and seer to the house of Israel, and through Israel to the whole world, is couched in the simple clause: "God created man in his own image" (Genesis 1:27; Pearl of Great Price—Book of Moses, 1:27–41).

The creation was two-fold—firstly spiritual, secondly temporal. This truth, also, Moses plainly taught—much more plainly than it has come down to us in the imperfect translations of the Bible that are now in use. Therein the fact of a spiritual creation, antedating the temporal creation, is strongly implied, but the proof of it is not so clear and conclusive as in other records held by the Latter-day Saints to be of equal authority with the Jewish scriptures. The partial obscurity of the latter upon the point in question is owing, no doubt, to the loss of those "plain and precious" parts of sacred writ, which, as the Book of Mormon informs us, have been taken away from the Bible during its passage down the centuries (I Nephi 13:24–29). Some of these missing parts the Prophet Joseph Smith undertook to restore when he revised those scriptures by the spirit of revelation, the result being that more complete account of the creation which is found in the Book of Moses, previously cited. Note the following passages:

> And now, behold, I say unto you, that these are the generations of the heaven and of the earth, when they were created, in the day that I, the Lord God, made the heaven and the earth;
>
> And every plant of the field before it was in the earth, and every herb of the field before it grew.

For I, the Lord God, created all things of which I have spoken, spiritually, before they were naturally upon the face of the earth. For I, the Lord God, had not caused it to rain upon the face of the earth.

And I, the Lord God, had created all the children of men, and not yet a man to till the ground; for in heaven created I them, and there was not yet flesh upon the earth, neither in the water, neither in the air.

But, I, the Lord God, spake, and there went up a mist from the earth, and watered the whole face of the ground.

And I, the Lord God, formed man from the dust of the ground, and breathed into his nostrils the breath of life; and man became a living soul, the first flesh upon the earth, the first man also.

Nevertheless, all things were before created, but spiritually were they created and made, according to my word (Pearl of Great Price—Book of Moses, 3:4–7. See also chapters 1 and 2, and compare with Genesis 1 and 2).

These two points being established, namely, the creation of man in the image of God, and the two-fold character of the creation, let us now inquire: What was the form of man, in the spirit and in the body, as originally created? In a general way the answer is given in the words chosen as the text of this treatise. "God created man in his own image." It is more explicitly rendered in the Book of Mormon thus: "All men were created in the beginning after mine own image" (Ether, 3:15). It is the Father who is speaking.[1] If, therefore, we can ascertain the form of the "Father of spirits," "The God of the spirits of all flesh," we shall be able to discover the form of the original man.

Jesus Christ, the Son of God, is "the express image" of His Father's person (Hebrews 1:3). He walked the earth as a human being, as a perfect man, and said, in answer to a question put to Him: "He that hath seen me hath seen the Father" (John 14:9).

---

1. The Book of Mormon seems to make clear that it is actually the Son who is speaking.

This alone ought to solve the problem to the satisfaction of every thoughtful, reverent mind. The conclusion is irresistible, that if the Son of God be the express image (that is, likeness) of His Father's person, then His Father is in the form of man; for that was the form of the Son of God, not only during His mortal life, but before His mortal birth, and after His resurrection. It was in this form that the Father and the Son, as two personages, appeared to Joseph Smith, when, as a boy of fourteen years, he received his first vision. Then if God made man—the first man—in His own image and likeness, he must have made him like unto Christ, and consequently like unto men of Christ's time and of the present day. That man was made in the image of Christ is positively stated in the Book of Moses: "And I, God, said unto mine Only Begotten, which was with me from the beginning, Let us make man in our image, after our likeness; and it was so.... And I, God, created man in mine own image, in the image of mine Only Begotten created I him, male and female created I them" (2:26, 27).

The Father of Jesus is our Father also. Jesus Himself taught this truth, when He instructed His disciples how to pray: "Our Father which art in heaven," etc. Jesus, however, is the firstborn among all the sons of God—the first begotten in the spirit, and the only begotten in the flesh. He is our elder brother, and we, like Him, are in the image of God. All men and women are in the similitude of the universal Father and Mother, and are literally the sons and daughters of Deity.

"God created man in His own image." This is just as true of the spirit as it is of the body, which is only the clothing of the spirit, its complement; the two together constituting the soul. The spirit of man is in the form of man, and the spirits of all creatures are in the likeness of their bodies. This was plainly taught by the Prophet Joseph Smith (Doctrine and Covenants, 77:2).

Here is further evidence of the fact. More than seven hundred years before Moses was shown the things pertaining to this earth, another great prophet, known to us as the brother of Jared, was similarly favored by the Lord. He was even permitted to behold the spirit-body of the foreordained Savior, prior to His incarnation; and so like the body of a man was gazing upon a being of flesh and blood. He first saw the finger and then the entire body of the Lord—all in the spirit. The Book of Mormon says of this wonderful manifestation:

> And it came to pass that when the brother of Jared had said these words, behold the Lord stretched forth His hand and touched the stones one by one with His finger; and the veil was taken from off the eyes of the brother of Jared, and he saw the finger of the Lord; and it was as the finger of a man, like unto flesh and blood; and the brother of Jared fell down before the Lord, for he was struck with fear.
>
> And the Lord saw that the brother of Jared had fallen to the earth; and the Lord said unto him, Arise, why hast thou fallen?
>
> And he saith unto the Lord, I saw the finger of the Lord, and I feared lest he should smite me; for I knew not that the Lord had flesh and blood.
>
> And the Lord said unto him, Because of thy faith thou hast seen that I shall take upon me flesh and blood; and never has man come before me with such exceeding faith as thou hast; for were it not so, ye could not have seen my finger. Sawest thou more than this?
>
> And he answered, Nay, Lord, show thyself unto me.
>
> And the Lord said unto him, Believest thou the words which I shall speak?
>
> And he answered, Yea, Lord, I know that thou speakest the truth, for thou art a God of truth and canst not lie.
>
> And when he had said these words, behold, the Lord showed himself unto him, and said, Because thou knowest these things ye are redeemed from the fall; therefore ye are brought back into my presence; therefore I show myself unto you.
>
> Behold, I am He who was prepared from the foundation of the world to redeem my people. Behold, I am Jesus Christ, I am the Father and the Son. In me shall all mankind have light, and that eternally, even they who shall believe on my name; and they shall become my sons and my daughters.

And never have I shewed myself unto man whom I have created, for never hath man believed in me as thou hast. Seest thou that ye are created after mine own image? Yea, even all men were created in the beginning after mine own image.

Behold, this body, which ye now behold, is the body of my spirit, and man have I created after the body of my spirit; and even as I appear unto thee to be in the spirit, will I appear unto my people in the flesh. (Ether, 3:6–16.)

What more is needed to convince us that man, both in spirit and in body, is the image and likeness of God, and that God Himself is in the form of man?

When the divine Being whose spirit-body the brother of Jared beheld, took upon Him flesh and blood, He appeared as a man, having "body, parts and passions," like other men, though vastly superior to all others, because He was God, even the Son of God, the Word made flesh: in Him "dwelt the fulness of the Godhead bodily." And why should He not appear as a man? That was the form of His spirit, and it must needs have an appropriate covering, a suitable tabernacle. He came unto the world as He had promised to come (III Nephi 1:13), taking an infant tabernacle, and developing it gradually to the fulness of His spirit stature. He came as man had been coming for ages, and as man has continued to come ever since. Jesus, however, as shown, was the only begotten of God in the flesh.

Adam, our great progenitor, "the first man," was, like Christ, a pre-existent spirit, and like Christ he took upon him an appropriate body, the body of a man, and so became a "living soul." The doctrine of the pre-existence,—revealed so plainly, particularly in latter days, pours a wonderful flood of light upon the otherwise mysterious problem of man's origin. It shows that man, as a spirit, was begotten and born of heavenly parents, and reared to maturity in the eternal mansions of the Father, prior to coming upon the earth in a temporal body to undergo an experience in mortality. It teaches that all men existed in the spirit

54

before any man existed in the flesh, and that all who have inhabited the earth since Adam have taken bodies and become souls in like manner.

It is held by some that Adam was not the first man upon this earth, and that the original human being was a development from lower orders of the animal creation. These, however, are the theories of men. The word of the Lord declares that Adam was "the first man of all men" (Moses 1:34), and we are therefore in duty bound to regard him as the primal parent of our race. It was shown to the brother of Jared that all men were created in the *beginning* after the image of God; and whether we take this to mean the spirit or the body, or both, it commits us to the same conclusion: Man began life as a human being, in the likeness of our heavenly Father.

True it is that the body of man enters upon its career as a tiny germ or embryo, which becomes an infant, quickened at a certain stage by the spirit whose tabernacle it is, and the child, after being born, develops into a man. There is nothing in this, however, to indicate that the original man, the first of our race, began life as anything less than a man, or less than the human germ or embryo that becomes a man.

Man, by searching, cannot find out God. Never, unaided, will he discover the truth about the beginning of human life. The Lord must reveal Himself, or remain unrevealed; and the same is true of the facts relating to the origin of Adam's race—God alone can reveal them. Some of these facts, however, are already known, and what has been made known it is our duty to receive and retain.

The Church of Jesus Christ of Latter-day Saints, basing its belief on divine revelation, ancient and modern, proclaims man to be the direct and lineal offspring of Deity. God Himself is an exalted man, perfected, enthroned, and supreme. By His almighty power He organized the earth, and all that it contains, from spirit and element, which exist co-eternally with Himself. He formed every plant that grows, and every animal that breathes, each after its own kind, spiritually and temporally—"that which is spiritual being in the likeness of that which is temporal, and that which is temporal in the likeness of that which is spiritual." He made the tadpole and the ape, the lion and the elephant but He did not make them in His own image, nor endow them with Godlike reason and intelligence. Nevertheless, the whole animal creation will be perfected and perpetuated in the Hereafter, each class in its "distinct order or sphere," and will enjoy "eternal felicity." That fact has been made plain in this dispensation (Doctrine and Covenants, 77:3).

Man is the child of God, formed in the divine image and endowed with divine attributes, and even as the infant son of an earthly father and mother is capable in due time of becoming a man, so the undeveloped offspring of celestial parentage is capable, by experience through ages and aeons, of evolving into a God.

Joseph F. Smith,
John R. Winder,
Anthon H. Lund,
First Presidency of The Church of Jesus Christ of Latter-day Saints.

The Lectures on Faith

On the Doctrine of The Church of Jesus Christ of
Latter-day Saints, originally delivered before a
Class of the Elders, in Kirtland, Ohio

LECTURE FIRST

1. Faith being the first principle in revealed religion, and the foundation of all righteousness, necessarily claims the first place in a course of lectures which are designed to unfold to the understanding the doctrine of Jesus Christ.

2. In presenting the subject of faith, we shall observe the following order—

3. First, faith itself—what it is.

4. Secondly, the object on which it rests. And,

5. Thirdly, the effects which flow from it.

6. Agreeable to this order we have first to show what faith is.

7. The author of the epistle to the Hebrews, in the eleventh chapter of that epistle and first verse, gives the following definition of the word faith:

8. "Now faith is the substance [assurance] of things hoped for, the evidence of things not seen."

9. From this we learn that faith is the assurance which men have of the existence of things which they have not seen, and the principle of action in all intelligent beings.

10. If men were duly to consider themselves, and turn their thoughts and reflections to the operations of their own minds,

they would readily discover that it is faith, and faith only, which is the moving cause of all action in them; that without it both mind and body would be in a state of inactivity, and all their exertions would cease, both physical and mental.

11. Were this class to go back and reflect upon the history of their lives, from the period of their first recollection, and ask themselves what principle excited them to action, or what gave them energy and activity in all their lawful avocations, callings, and pursuits, what would be the answer? Would it not be that it was the assurance which they had of the existence of things which they had not seen as yet? Was it not the hope which you had, in consequence of your belief in the existence of unseen things, which stimulated you to action and exertion in order to obtain them? Are you not dependent on your faith, or belief, for the acquisition of all knowledge, wisdom, and intelligence? Would you exert yourselves to obtain wisdom and intelligence, unless you did believe that you could obtain them? Would you have ever sown, if you had not believed that you would reap? Would you have ever planted, if you had not believed that you would gather? Would you have ever asked, unless you had believed that you would receive? Would you have ever sought unless you had believed that you would have found? Or, would you have ever knocked, unless you had believed that it would have been opened unto you? In a word, is there anything that you would have done, either physical or mental, if you had not previously believed? Are not all your exertions of every kind, dependent on your faith? Or, may we not ask, what have you, or what do you possess, which you have not obtained by reason of your faith? Your food, your raiment, your lodgings, are they not all by reason of your faith? Reflect, and ask yourselves if these things are not so. Turn your thoughts on your own minds, and see if faith is not the moving cause of all action in yourselves; and, if the moving cause in you, is it not in all other intelligent beings?

12. And as faith is the moving cause of all action in temporal concerns, so it is in spiritual; for the Saviour has said, and that truly, that "He that *believeth* and is baptized shall be saved." (Mark 16:16; italics added.)

13. As we receive by faith all temporal blessings that we do receive, so we in like manner receive by faith all spiritual blessings that we do receive. But faith is not only the principle of action, but of power also, in all intelligent beings, whether in heaven or on earth. Thus says the author of the epistle to the Hebrews (11:3):

14. "Through faith we understand that the worlds were framed by the word of God, so that things which are seen were not made of things which do appear."

15. By this we understand that the principle of power which existed in the bosom of God, by which the worlds were framed, was faith; and that it is by reason of this principle of power existing in the Deity, that all created things exist; so that all things in heaven, on earth, or under the earth, exist by reason of faith as it existed in HIM.

16. Had it not been for the principle of faith the worlds would never have been framed, neither would man have been formed of the dust. It is the principle by which Jehovah works, and through which he exercises power over all temporal as well as eternal things. Take this principle or attribute—for it is an attribute—from the Deity, and he would cease to exist.

17. Who cannot see, that if God framed the worlds by faith, that it is by faith that he exercises power over them, and that faith is the principle of power? And if the principle of power, it must be so in man as well as in the Deity? This is the testimony of all the sacred writers, and the lesson which they have been endeavouring to teach to man.

18. The Saviour says (Matt.17:19–20), in explaining the reason why the disciples could not cast out the devil, that it was because of their unbelief: "For verily I say unto you," said he, "If ye have faith as a grain of mustard seed, ye shall say unto this mountain, Remove hence to yonder place, and it shall remove; and nothing shall be impossible unto you."

19. Moroni, while abridging and compiling the record of his fathers, has given us the following account of faith as the principle of power. He says, [Ether 12:13], that it was the faith of Alma and Amulek which caused the walls of the prison to be

rent, as recorded [in Alma 14:23–29]; it was the faith of Nephi and Lehi which caused a change to be wrought upon the hearts of the Lamanites, when they were immersed with the Holy Spirit and with fire, as seen [in Helaman 5:37–50]; and that it was by faith the mountain Zerin was removed when the brother of Jared spake in the name of the Lord. See also [Ether 12:30].

20. In addition to this we are told in Hebrews 11:32–35, that Gideon, Barak, Samson, Jephthah, David, Samuel, and the prophets, through faith subdued kingdoms, wrought righteousness, obtained promises, stopped the mouths of lions, quenched the violence of fire, escaped the edge of the sword; out of weakness were made strong, waxed valiant in fight, turned to flight the armies of the aliens, and that women received their dead raised to life again, &c., &c.

21. Also Joshua, in the sight of all Israel, bade the sun and moon to stand still, and it was done. (Josh. 10:12–13.)

22. We here understand, that the sacred writers say that all these things were done by faith. It was by faith that the worlds were framed. God spake, chaos heard, and worlds came into order by reason of the faith there was in HIM. So with man also; he spake by faith in the name of God, and the sun stood still, the moon obeyed, mountains removed, prisons fell, lions' mouths were closed, the human heart lost its enmity, fire its violence, armies their power, the sword its terror, and death its dominion; and all this by reason of the faith which was in him.

23. Had it not been for the faith which was in men, they might have spoken to the sun, the moon, the mountains, prisons, the human heart, fire, armies, the sword, or to death in vain!

24. Faith, then, is the first great governing principle which has power, dominion, and authority over all things; by it they exist, by it they are upheld, by it they are changed, or by it they remain, agreeable to the will of God. Without it there is no power, and without power there could be no creation nor existence!

Questions and Answers on the Foregoing Principles

What is theology? It is that revealed science which treats of the being and attributes of God, his relations to us, the dispensations of his providence, his will with respect to our actions, and his purposes with respect to our end. (*Buck's Theological Dictionary,* page 582.)

What is the first principle in this revealed science? Faith. (Lecture 1:1.)

Why is faith the first principle in this revealed science? Because it is the foundation of all righteousness. Hebrews 11:6: "Without faith it is impossible to please [God]." 1 John 3:7: "Little children, let no man deceive you: he that doeth righteousness is righteous, even as he [God] is righteous." (Lecture 1:1.)

What arrangement should be followed in presenting the subject of faith? First, it should be shown what faith is. (Lecture 1:3.) Secondly, the object upon which it rests. (Lecture 1:4.) And, thirdly, the effects which flow from it. (Lecture 1:5.)

What is faith? It is the assurance of things hoped for, the evidence of things not seen (Heb. 11:1); that is, it is the assurance we have of the existence of unseen things. And being the assurance which we have of the existence of unseen things, must be the principle of action in all intelligent beings. Hebrews 11:3: "Through faith we understand that the worlds were framed by the word of God." (Lecture 1:8–9.)

How do you prove that faith is the principle of action in all intelligent beings? First, by duly considering the operations of my own mind; and, secondly, by the direct declaration of Scripture. Hebrews 11:7: "By faith Noah, being warned of God of things not seen as yet, moved with fear, prepared an ark to the saving of his house; by the which he condemned the world, and became heir of the righteousness which is by faith." Hebrews 11:8: "By faith Abraham, when he was called to go out into a place which he should after receive for an inheritance, obeyed; and he went out, not knowing whither he went." Hebrews 11:9: "By faith he sojourned in the land of promise, as in a strange country, dwelling in tabernacles with Isaac and Jacob, the heirs with him of the same promise." Hebrews 11:27: By faith Moses "forsook Egypt, not fearing the wrath of the king: for he endured, as seeing him who is invisible." (Lecture 1:10–11.)

Is not faith the principle of action in spiritual things as well as in temporal? It is.

How do you prove it? Hebrews 11:6: "Without faith it is impossible to please [God]." Mark 16:16: "He that believeth and is baptized shall be saved." Romans 4:16: "Therefore it is of faith, that it might be by grace; to the end the promise might be sure to all the seed; not to that only which is of the law, but to that also which is of the faith of Abraham; who is the father of us all." (Lecture 1:12–13.)

Is faith anything else beside the principle of action? It is.

What is it? It is the principle of power also. (Lecture 1:13.)

How do you prove it? First, it is the principle of power in the Deity as well as in man. Hebrews 11:3: "Through faith we understand that the worlds were framed by the word of God, so that things which are seen were not made of things which do appear." (Lecture 1:14–16.) Secondly, it is the principle of power in man also. Book of Mormon, [Alma 14:23–29]: Alma and Amulek are delivered from prison. [Helaman 5:37–50]: Nephi and Lehi, with the Lamanites, are immersed with the Spirit. [Ether 12:30]: The mountain Zerin, by the faith of the brother of Jared, is removed. Joshua 10:12: "Then spake Joshua to the Lord in the day when the Lord delivered up the Amorites before the children of Israel, and he said in the sight of Israel, Sun, stand thou still upon Gibeon; and thou, Moon, in the valley of Ajalon." Joshua 10:13: "And the sun stood still, and the moon stayed, until the people had avenged themselves upon their enemies. Is not this written in the book of Jasher? So the sun stood still in the midst of heaven, and hasted not to go down about a whole day." Matthew 17:19: "Then came the disciples to Jesus apart, and said, Why could not we cast him out?" Matthew 17:20: "And Jesus said unto them, Because of your unbelief; for verily I say unto you, if ye have faith as a grain of mustard seed, ye shall say unto this mountain, Remove hence to yonder place; and it shall remove; and nothing shall be impossible unto you." Hebrews 11:32 and the following verses: "And what shall I more say? for the time would fail me to tell of Gideon, and of Barak, and of Samson, and of Jephthae, of David also, and Samuel, and of the prophets: who through faith subdued kingdoms, wrought righteousness, obtained promises, stopped the mouths of lions, quenched the violence of fire, escaped the edge of the sword, out of weakness were made strong, waxed valiant in fight, turned to flight the armies of the aliens. Women received their dead raised to life again, and others were tortured, not accepting deliverance; that they might obtain a better resurrection." (Lecture 1:16–22.)

How would you define faith in its most unlimited sense? It is the first great governing principle which has power, dominion, and authority over all things. (Lecture 1:24.)

How do you convey to the understanding more clearly that faith is the first great governing principle which has power, dominion, and authority over all things? By it they exist, by it they are upheld, by it they are changed, or by it they remain, agreeable to the will of God; and without it there is no power, and without power there could be no creation nor existence! (Lecture 1:24.)

LECTURE SECOND

1. Having shown in our previous lecture "faith itself—what it is," we shall proceed to show, secondly, the object on which it rests.

2. We here observe that God is the only supreme governor and independent being in whom all fullness and perfection dwell; who is omnipotent, omnipresent, and omniscient; without beginning of days or end of life; and that in him every good gift and every good principle dwell; and that he is the Father of lights; in him the principle of faith dwells independently, and he is the object in whom the faith of all other rational and accountable beings center for life and salvation.

3. In order to present this part of the subject in a clear and conspicuous point of light, it is necessary to go back and show the evidences which mankind have had, and the foundation on which these evidences are, or were, based since the creation, to believe in the existence of a God.

4. We do not mean those evidences which are manifested by the works of creation which we daily behold with our natural eyes. We are sensible that, after a revelation of Jesus Christ,

the works of creation, throughout their vast forms and varieties, clearly exhibit his eternal power and Godhead. Romans 1:20: "For the invisible things of him from the creation of the world are clearly seen, being understood by the things that are made, even his eternal power and Godhead;" but we mean those evidences by which the first thoughts were suggested to the minds of men that there was a God who created all things.

5. We shall now proceed to examine the situation of man at his first creation. Moses, the historian, has given us the following account of him in the first chapter of the book of Genesis, beginning with the 20th verse, and closing with the 30th.[1] We copy from the new translation:

6. "And I, God, said unto mine Only Begotten, which was with me from the beginning, Let us make man in our image, after our likeness; and it was so.

7. "And I, God, said, Let them have dominion over the fishes of the sea, and over the fowl of the air, and over the cattle, and over all the earth, and over every creeping thing that creepeth upon the earth.

8. "And I, God, created man in mine own image, in the image of mine Only Begotten created I him; male and female created I them. And I, God, blessed them, and said unto them, Be fruitful, and multiply, and replenish the earth, and subdue it; and have dominion over the fish of the sea, and over the fowl of the air, and over every living thing that moveth upon the earth.

9. "And I, God, said unto man, Behold, I have given you every herb, bearing seed, which is upon the face of all the earth, and every tree in the which shall be the fruit of a tree, yielding seed; to you it shall be for meat."

10. Again, Genesis 2:15–17, 19–20:[2] "And I, the Lord God, took the man, and put him into the garden of Eden, to dress it, and to keep it. And I, the Lord God, commanded the man, saying, Of every tree of the garden thou mayest freely eat; but of the tree of the knowledge of good and evil, thou shalt not eat of it;

---

1. See Joseph Smith Translation, Genesis 1:27–31; Moses 2:26–29.
2. Joseph Smith Translation, Genesis 2:18–22, 25–27; Moses 3:15–17, 19–20.

nevertheless thou mayest choose for thyself, for it is given unto thee; but remember that I forbid it; for in the day thou eatest thereof thou shalt surely die. . . .

11. "And out of the ground, I, the Lord God, formed every beast of the field, and every fowl of the air; and commanded that they should come unto Adam, to see what he would call them. And . . . whatsoever Adam called every living creature, that should be the name thereof. And Adam gave names to all cattle, and to the fowl of the air, and to every beast of the field."

12. From the foregoing we learn man's situation at his first creation, the knowledge with which he was endowed, and the high and exalted station in which he was placed—lord or governor of all things on earth, and at the same time enjoying communion and intercourse with his Maker, without a vail to separate between. We shall next proceed to examine the account given of his fall, and of his being driven out of the garden of Eden, and from the presence of the Lord.

13. Moses proceeds: "And they [Adam and Eve] heard the voice of the Lord God, as they were walking in the garden, in the cool of the day. And Adam and his wife went to hide themselves from the presence of the Lord God, amongst the trees of the garden. And I, the Lord God, called unto Adam, and said unto him, Where goest thou? And he said, I heard thy voice, in the garden, and I was afraid, because I beheld that I was naked, and I hid myself.

14. "And I, the Lord God, said unto Adam, Who told thee that thou wast naked? Hast thou eaten of the tree whereof I commanded thee that thou shouldst not eat, if so, thou shouldst surely die? And the man said, The woman whom thou gavest me, and commanded that she should remain with me, gave me of the fruit of the tree, and I did eat.

15. "And I, the Lord God, said unto the woman, What is this thing which thou hast done? And the woman said, The serpent beguiled me, and I did eat."[3]

---

3. Joseph Smith Translation, Genesis 3:13–19; Moses 4:14–19.

16. And again, the Lord said unto the woman, "I will greatly multiply thy sorrow, and thy conception; in sorrow thou shalt bring forth children, and thy desire shall be to thy husband, and he shall rule over thee.

17. "And unto Adam, I, the Lord God, said, Because thou hast hearkened unto the voice of thy wife, and hast eaten of the fruit of the tree, of which I commanded thee, saying, Thou shalt not eat of it, cursed shall be the ground for thy sake; in sorrow shalt thou eat of it all the days of thy life; thorns also and thistles shall it bring forth to thee; and thou shalt eat the herb of the field; by the sweat of thy face shalt thou eat bread, until thou shalt return unto the ground, for thou shalt surely die; for out of it wast thou taken, for dust thou wast, and unto dust shalt thou return."[4] This was immediately followed by the fulfillment of what was previously said—Man was driven or sent out of Eden.

18. Two important items are shown from the former quotations. First, after man was created, he was not left without intelligence or understanding, to wander in darkness and spend an existence in ignorance and doubt (on the great and important point which effected his happiness) as to the real fact by whom he was created, or unto whom he was amenable for his conduct. God conversed with him face to face. In his presence he was permitted to stand, and from his own mouth he was permitted to receive instruction. He heard his voice, walked before him and gazed upon his glory, while intelligence burst upon his understanding, and enabled him to give names to the vast assemblage of his Maker's works.

19. Secondly, we have seen, that though man did transgress, his transgression did not deprive him of the previous knowledge with which he was endowed relative to the existence and glory of his Creator; for no sooner did he hear his voice than he sought to hide himself from his presence.

20. Having shown, then, in the first instance, that God began to converse with man immediately after he "breathed into his nostrils the breath of life," and that he did not cease to manifest

---

4. Joseph Smith Translation, Genesis 3:22–25; Moses 4:22–25.

himself to him, even after his fall, we shall next proceed to show, that though he was cast out from the garden of Eden, his knowledge of the existence of God was not lost, neither did God cease to manifest his will unto him.

21. We next proceed to present the account of the direct revelation which man received after he was cast out of Eden, and further copy from the new translation:

22. After Adam had been driven out of the garden, he "began to till the earth, and to have dominion over all the beasts of the field, and to eat his bread by the sweat of his brow, as I, the Lord had commanded him." And he called upon the name of the Lord, and so did Eve, his wife, also. "And they heard the voice of the Lord, from the way towards the garden of Eden, speaking unto them, and they saw him not; for they were shut out from his presence. And he gave unto them commandments, that they should worship the Lord their God; and should offer the firstlings of their flocks for an offering unto the Lord. And Adam was obedient unto the commandments of the Lord.

23. "And after many days, an angel of the Lord appeared unto Adam, saying, Why dost thou offer sacrifices unto the Lord? And Adam said unto him, I know not, save the Lord commanded me.

24. "And then the angel spake, saying, This thing is a similitude of the sacrifice of the Only Begotten of the Father, which is full of grace and truth; wherefore, thou shalt do all that thou doest, in the name of the Son. And thou shalt repent, and call upon God, in the name of the Son for evermore. And in that day, the Holy Ghost fell upon Adam, which beareth record of the Father and the Son."[5]

25. This last quotation, or summary, shows this important fact, that though our first parents were driven out of the garden of Eden, and were even separated from the presence of God by a vail, they still retained a knowledge of his existence, and that sufficiently to move them to call upon him. And further, that no sooner was the plan of redemption revealed to man, and he

---

5. Joseph Smith Translation, Genesis 4:1, 4–9; Moses 5:1, 4–9.

began to call upon God, than the Holy Spirit was given, bearing record of the Father and Son.

26. Moses also gives us an account, in the fourth of Genesis, of the transgression of Cain, and the righteousness of Abel, and of the revelations of God to them.[6] He says, "In process of time . . . Cain brought of the fruit of the ground an offering unto the Lord. And Abel, he also brought, of the firstlings of his flock, and of the fat thereof; and the Lord had respect unto Abel, and to his offering, but unto Cain, and to his offering he had not respect. Now Satan knew this, and it pleased him. And Cain was very wroth, and his countenance fell. And the Lord said unto Cain, Why art thou wroth? Why is thy countenance fallen? If thou doest well thou shalt be accepted, and if thou doest not well, sin lieth at the door; and Satan desireth to have thee, and except thou shalt hearken unto my commandments, I will deliver thee up, and it shall be unto thee according to his desire. . . .

27. "And Cain went into the field, and Cain talked with Abel his brother; and it came to pass, that while they were in the field Cain rose up against Abel his brother, and slew him. And Cain gloried in that which he had done, saying, I am free; surely the flocks of my brother falleth into my hands.

28. "And the Lord said unto Cain, Where is Abel, thy brother? And he said, I know not, am I my brother's keeper? And the Lord said, What hast thou done? The voice of thy brother's blood cries unto me from the ground. And now, thou shalt be cursed from the earth, which hath opened her mouth to receive thy brother's blood from thy hand. When thou tillest the ground, it shall not henceforth yield unto thee her strength; a fugitive and a vagabond shalt thou be in the earth.

29. "And Cain said unto the Lord, Satan tempted me, because of my brother's flocks; and I was wroth also, for his offering thou didst accept, and not mine. My punishment is greater than I can bear. Behold, thou hast driven me out this day from the face of the Lord, and from thy face shall I be hid; and I shall be a fugitive and a vagabond in the earth; and it shall come to pass, that

---

6. Joseph Smith Translation, Genesis 5:6–9, 17–25; Moses 5:19–23, 32–40.

he that findeth me shall slay me, because of mine iniquities, for these things are not hid from the Lord. And I, the Lord, said unto him, Whosoever slayeth thee, vengeance shall be taken on him seven-fold; and I, the Lord, set a mark upon Cain, lest any finding him should kill him."

30. The object of the foregoing quotations is to show to this class the way by which mankind were first made acquainted with the existence of a God; that it was by a manifestation of God to man, and that God continued, after man's transgression, to manifest himself to him and to his posterity; and, notwithstanding they were separated from his immediate presence that they could not see his face, they continued to hear his voice.

31. Adam, thus being made acquainted with God, communicated the knowledge which he had unto his posterity; and it was through this means that the thought was first suggested to their minds that there was a God, which laid the foundation for the exercise of their faith, through which they could obtain a knowledge of his character and also of his glory.

32. Not only was there a manifestation made unto Adam of the existence of a God; but Moses informs us, as before quoted, that God condescended to talk with Cain after his great transgression in slaying his brother, and that Cain knew that it was the Lord that was talking with him, so that when he was driven out from the presence of his brethren, he carried with him the knowledge of the existence of a God; and, through this means, doubtless, his posterity became acquainted with the fact that such a Being existed.

33. From this we can see that the whole human family in the early age of their existence, in all their different branches, had this knowledge disseminated among them; so that the existence of God became an object of faith in the early age of the world. And the evidences which these men had of the existence of a God, was the testimony of their fathers in the first instance.

34. The reason why we have been thus particular on this part of our subject, is that this class may see by what means it was that God became an object of faith among men after the fall; and what it was that stirred up the faith of multitudes to feel after

him—to search after a knowledge of his character, perfections and attributes, until they became extensively acquainted with him, and not only commune with him and behold his glory, but be partakers of his power and stand in his presence.

35. Let this class mark particularly, that the testimony which these men had of the existence of a God, was the testimony of man; for previous to the time that any of Adam's posterity had obtained a manifestation of God to themselves, Adam, their common father, had testified unto them of the existence of God, and of his eternal power and Godhead.

36. For instance, Abel, before he received the assurance from heaven that his offerings were acceptable unto God, had received the important information of his father that such a Being did exist, who had created and who did uphold all things. Neither can there be a doubt existing on the mind of any person, that Adam was the first who did communicate the knowledge of the existence of a God to his posterity; and that the whole faith of the world, from that time down to the present is in a certain degree dependent on the knowledge first communicated to them by their common progenitor; and it has been handed down to the day and generation in which we live, as we shall show from the face of the sacred records.

37. First, Adam was 130 years old when Seth was born. (Genesis 5:3.) And the days of Adam, after he had begotten Seth, were 800 years, making him 930 years old when he died. (Genesis 5:4–5.) Seth was 105 when Enos was born (v. 6); Enos was 90 when Cainan was born (v. 9); Cainan was 70 when Mahalaleel was born (v.12); Mahalaleel was 65 when Jared was born (v. 15); Jared was 162 when Enoch was born (v. 18); Enoch was 65 when Methuselah was born (v. 21); Methuselah was 187 when Lamech was born (v. 25); Lamech was 182 when Noah was born (v. 28).

38. From this account it appears that Lamech, the 9th from Adam, and the father of Noah, was 56 years old when Adam died; Methuselah, 243; Enoch, 308; Jared, 470; Mahalaleel, 535; Cainan, 605; Enos, 695; and Seth, 800.

39. So that Lamech the father of Noah, Methuselah, Enoch, Jared, Mahalaleel, Cainan, Enos, Seth, and Adam, were all living

at the same time, and, beyond all controversy, were all preachers of righteousness.

40. Moses further informs us that Seth lived after he begat Enos, 807 years, making him 912 years old at his death. (Gen. 5:7–8.) And Enos lived after he begat Cainan, 815 years, making him 905 years old when he died (vv. 10–11.) And Cainan lived after he begat Mahalaleel, 840 years, making him 910 years old at his death (vv. 13–14.) And Mahalaleel lived after he begat Jared, 830 years, making him 895 years old when he died (vv. 16–17.) And Jared lived after he begat Enoch, 800 years, making him 962 years old at his death (vv. 19–20.) And Enoch walked with God after he begat Methuselah 300 years, making him 365 years old when he was translated (vv. 22–23.)[7] And Methuselah lived after he begat Lamech, 782 years, making him 969 years old when he died (vv. 26–27.) Lamech lived after he begat Noah, 595 years, making him 777 years old when he died (vv. 30–31.)

41. Agreeable to this account, Adam died in the 930th year of the world; Enoch was translated in the 987th,[8] Seth died in the 1042nd; Enos in the 1140th; Cainan in the 1235th; Mahalaleel in the 1290th; Jared in the 1422nd; Lamech in the 1651st; and Methuselah in the 1656th, it being the same year in which the flood came.

42. So that Noah was 84 years old when Enos died, 176 when Cainan died, 234 when Mahalaleel died, 366 when Jared died, 595 when Lamech died, and 600 when Methuselah died.

43. We can see from this that Enos, Cainan, Mahalaleel, Jared, Methuselah, Lamech, and Noah, all lived on the earth at the same time; and that Enos, Cainan, Mahalaleel, Jared, Methuselah, and Lamech, were all acquainted with both Adam and Noah.

---

7. Orson Pratt, when he edited the Doctrine and Covenants in 1879, added this footnote: "According to the Old Testament. For Enoch's age, see Covenants and Commandments, Section 107:49."

8. Orson Pratt, when he edited the Doctrine and Covenants in 1879, added this footnote: "According to the Old Testament. For Enoch's age, see Covenants and Commandments, Section 107:49."

44. From the foregoing it is easily to be seen, not only how the knowledge of God came into the world, but upon what principle it was preserved; that from the time it was first communicated, it was retained in the minds of righteous men, who taught not only their own posterity but the world; so that there was no need of a new revelation to man, after Adam's creation to Noah, to give them the first idea or notion of the existence of a God; and not only of a God, but the true and living God.

45. Having traced the chronology of the world from Adam to Noah, we will now trace it from Noah to Abraham. Noah was 502 years old when Shem was born; 98 years afterwards the flood came, being the 600th year of Noah's age. And Moses informs us that Noah lived after the flood 350 years, making him 950 years old when he died. (Gen. 9:28–29.)

46. Shem was 100 years old when Arphaxad was born. (Gen. 11:10.) Arphaxad was 35 when Salah was born (11:12); Salah was 30 when Eber was born (11:14); Eber was 34 when Peleg was born, in whose days the earth was divided (11:16); Peleg was 30 when Reu was born (11:18); Reu was 32 when Serug was born (11:20); Serug was 30 when Nahor was born (11:22); Nahor was 29 when Terah was born (11:24); Terah was 70 when Haran and Abraham were born (11:26).

47. There is some difficulty in the account given by Moses of Abraham's birth. Some have supposed that Abraham was not born until Terah was 130 years old. This conclusion is drawn from a variety of scriptures, which are not to our purpose at present to quote. Neither is it a matter of any consequence to us whether Abraham was born when Terah was 70 years old, or 130. But in order that there may no doubt exist upon any mind in relation to the object lying immediately before us, in presenting the present chronology we will date the birth of Abraham at the latest period, that is, when Terah was 130 years old. It appears from this account that from the flood to the birth of Abraham, was 352 years.

48. Moses informs us that Shem lived after he begat Arphaxad, 500 years (11:11); this added to 100 years, which was his age when Arphaxad was born, makes him 600 years old

when he died. Arphaxad lived after he begat Salah, 403 years (11:13); this added to 35 years, which was his age when Salah was born, makes him 438 years old when he died. Salah lived after he begat Eber, 403 years (11:15); this added to 30 years, which was his age when Eber was born, makes him 433 years old when he died. Eber lived after he begat Peleg, 430 years (11:17); this added to 34 years, which was his age when Peleg was born, makes him 464 years old. Peleg lived after he begat Reu, 209 years (11:19); this added to 30 years, which was his age when Reu was born, makes him 239 years old when he died. Reu lived after he begat Serug 207 years (11:21); this added to 32 years, which was his age when Serug was born, makes him 239 years old when he died. Serug lived after he begat Nahor, 200 years (11:23); this added to 30 years, which was his age when Nahor was born, makes him 230 years old when he died. Nahor lived after he begat Terah, 119 years (11:25); this added to 29 years, which was his age when Terah was born, makes him 148 years old when he died. Terah was 130 years old when Abraham was born, and is supposed to have lived 75 years after his birth, making him 205 years old when he died.

49. Agreeable to this last account, Peleg died in the 1996th year of the world, Nahor in the 1997th, and Noah in the 2006th. So that Peleg, in whose days the earth was divided, and Nahor, the grandfather of Abraham, both died before Noah—the former being 239 years old, and the latter 148; and who cannot but see that they must have had a long and intimate acquaintance with Noah?

50. Reu died in the 2026th year of the world, Serug in the 2049th, Terah in the 2083rd, Arphaxad in the 2096th, Salah in the 2126th, Shem in the 2158th, Abraham in the 2183rd, and Eber in the 2187th, which was four years after Abraham's death. And Eber was the fourth from Noah.

51. Nahor, Abraham's brother, was 58 years old when Noah died, Terah 128, Serug 187, Reu 219, Eber 283, Salah 313, Arphaxad 344, and Shem 448.

52. It appears from this account, that Nahor, brother of Abraham, Terah, Nahor, Serug, Reu, Peleg, Eber, Salah, Arphaxad,

Shem, and Noah, all lived on the earth at the same time; and that Abraham was 18 years old when Reu died, 41 when Serug and his brother Nahor died, 75 when Terah died, 88 when Arphaxad died, 118 when Salah died, 150 when Shem died, and that Eber lived four years after Abraham's death. And that Shem, Arphaxad, Salah, Eber, Reu, Serug, Terah, and Nahor, the brother of Abraham, and Abraham, lived at the same time. And that Nahor, brother of Abraham, Terah, Serug, Reu, Eber, Salah, Arphaxad, and Shem, were all acquainted with both Noah and Abraham.

53. We have now traced the chronology of the world agreeable to the account given in our present Bible, from Adam to Abraham, and have clearly determined, beyond the power of controversy, that there was no difficulty in preserving the knowledge of God in the world from the creation of Adam, and the manifestation made to his immediate descendants, as set forth in the former part of this lecture; so that the students in this class need not have any doubt resting on their minds on this subject, for they can easily see that it is impossible for it to be otherwise, but that the knowledge of the existence of a God must have continued from father to son, as a matter of tradition at least; for we cannot suppose that a knowledge of this important fact could have existed in the mind of any of the before-mentioned individuals, without their having made it known to their posterity.

54. We have now shown how it was that the first thought ever existed in the mind of any individual that there was such a Being as a God, who had created and did uphold all things: that it was by reason of the manifestation which he first made to our father Adam, when he stood in his presence, and conversed with him face to face, at the time of his creation.

55. Let us here observe, that after any portion of the human family are made acquainted with the important fact that there is a God, who has created and does uphold all things, the extent of their knowledge respecting his character and glory will depend upon their diligence and faithfulness in seeking after him, until, like Enoch, the brother of Jared, and Moses, they shall obtain faith in God, and power with him to behold him face to face.

56. We have now clearly set forth how it is, and how it was, that God became an object of faith for rational beings; and also, upon what foundation the testimony was based which excited the inquiry and diligent search of the ancient saints to seek after and obtain a knowledge of the glory of God; and we have seen that it was human testimony, and human testimony only, that excited this inquiry, in the first instance, in their minds. It was the credence they gave to the testimony of their fathers, this testimony having aroused their minds to inquire after the knowledge of God; the inquiry frequently terminated, indeed always terminated when rightly pursued, in the most glorious discoveries and eternal certainty.

Questions and Answers on the Foregoing Principles

Is there a being who has faith in himself, independently? There is. *Who is it?* It is God.

How do you prove that God has faith in himself independently? Because he is omnipotent, omnipresent, and omniscient; without beginning of days or end of life, and in him all fullness dwells. Ephesians 1:23: "Which is his body, the fulness of him that filleth all in all." Colossians 1:19: "For it pleased the Father that in him should all fulness dwell." (Lecture 2:2.)

Is he the object in whom the faith of all other rational and accountable beings center, for life and salvation? He is.

How do you prove it? Isaiah 45:22: "Look unto me, and be ye saved, all the ends of the earth: for I am God, and there is none else." Romans 11:34–36: "For who hath known the mind of the Lord? or who hath been his counsellor? or who hath first given to him, and it shall be recompensed unto him again? For of him, and through him, and to him, are all things: to whom be glory for ever. Amen." Isaiah 40, from the 9th to the 18th verses: "O Zion, that bringest good tidings [or, O thou that tellest good tidings to Zion], get thee up into the high mountain; O Jerusalem, that bringest good tidings [or, O thou that tellest good tidings to Jerusalem], lift up thy voice with strength; lift it up, be not afraid; say unto the cities of Judah, Behold your God! Behold, the Lord

God will come with strong hand [or, against the strong], and his arm shall rule for him: behold, his reward is with him, and his work before him [or, recompense for his work]. He shall feed his flock like a shepherd: he shall gather the lambs with his arm, and carry them in his bosom, and shall gently lead those that are with young. Who hath measured the waters in the hollow of his hand, and meted out heaven with the span, and comprehended the dust of the earth in a measure, and weighed the mountains in scales, and the hills in a balance? Who hath directed the Spirit of the Lord, or being his counsellor hath taught him? With whom took he counsel, and who instructed him, and taught him in the path of judgment, and taught him knowledge, and shewed to him the way of understanding? Behold, the nations are as a drop of a bucket, and are counted as the small dust of the balance: behold, he taketh up the isles as a very little thing. And Lebanon is not sufficient to burn, nor the beasts thereof sufficient for a burnt offering. All nations before him are as nothing; and they are counted to him less than nothing, and vanity." Jeremiah 51:15–16: "He [the Lord] hath made the earth by his power, he hath established the world by his wisdom, and hath stretched out the heaven by his understanding. When he uttereth his voice, there is a multitude of waters in the heavens; and he causeth the vapours to ascend from the ends of the earth: he maketh lightnings with rain, and bringeth forth the wind out of his treasures." 1 Corinthians 8:6: "But to us there is but one God, the Father, of whom are all things, and we in him; and one Lord Jesus Christ, by whom are all things, and we by him." (Lecture 2:2.)

How did men first come to the knowledge of the existence of a God, so as to exercise faith in him? In order to answer this question, it will be necessary to go back and examine man at his creation; the circumstances in which he was placed, and the knowledge which he had of God. (Lecture 2:3–11.) First, when man was created he stood in the presence of God. (Gen. 1:27–28.) From this we learn that man, at his creation, stood in the presence of his God, and had most perfect knowledge of his existence. Secondly, God conversed with him after his transgression. (Gen. 3: from the 8th to the 22nd; Lecture 2:13–17.) From this we learn that, though man did transgress, he was not deprived of the previous knowledge which he had of the existence of God. (Lecture 2:19.) Thirdly, God conversed with man after he cast him out of the garden. (Lecture 2:22–25.) Fourthly, God also conversed with Cain after he had slain Abel. (Gen. 4: from the 4th to the 6th; Lecture 2:26–29.)

What is the object of the foregoing quotation? It is that it may be clearly seen how it was that the first thoughts were suggested to the minds of men of the existence of God, and how extensively this knowledge was spread among the immediate descendants of Adam. (Lecture 2:30–33.)

What testimony had the immediate descendants of Adam, in proof of the existence of God? The testimony of their father. And after they were made acquainted with his existence, by the testimony of their father, they were dependent upon the exercise of their own faith, for a knowledge of his character, perfections, and attributes. (Lecture 2:23–26.)

Had any other of the human family, besides Adam, a knowledge of the existence of God, in the first instance, by any other means than human testimony? They had not. For previous to the time that they could have power to obtain a manifestation for themselves, the all-important fact had been communicated to them by their common father; and so from father to child the knowledge was communicated as extensively as the knowledge of his existence was known; for it was by this means, in the first instance, that men had a knowledge of his existence. (Lecture 2:35–36.)

How do you know that the knowledge of the existence of God was communicated in this manner, throughout the different ages of the world? By the chronology obtained through the revelations of God.

How would you divide that chronology in order to convey it to the understanding clearly? Into two parts—First, by embracing that period of the world from Adam to Noah; and secondly, from Noah to Abraham; from which period the knowledge of the existence of God has been so general, that it is a matter of no dispute in what manner the idea of his existence has been retained in the world.

How many noted righteous men lived from Adam to Noah? Nine; which includes Abel, who was slain by his brother.

What are their names? Abel, Seth, Enos, Cainan, Mahalaleel, Jared, Enoch, Methuselah, and Lamech.

How old was Adam when Seth was born? One hundred and thirty years. (Gen. 5:3.)

How many years did Adam live after Seth was born? Eight hundred. (Gen. 5:4.)

How old was Adam when he died? Nine hundred and thirty years. (Gen. 5:5.)

How old was Seth when Enos was born? One hundred and five years. (Gen. 5:6.)

How old was Enos when Cainan was born? Ninety years. (Gen. 5:9.)

How old was Cainan when Mahalaleel was born? Seventy years. (Gen. 5:12.)

How old was Mahalaleel when Jared was born? Sixty-five years. (Gen. 5:15.)

How old was Jared when Enoch was born? One hundred and sixty-two years. (Gen. 5:18.)

How old was Enoch when Methuselah was born? Sixty-five years. (Gen. 5:21.)

How old was Methuselah when Lamech was born? One hundred and eighty-seven years. (Gen. 5:25.)

How old was Lamech when Noah was born? One hundred and eighty-two years. (Gen. 5:28.) For this chronology, see Lecture 2:37.

How many years, according to this account, was it from Adam to Noah? One thousand and fifty-six years.

How old was Lamech when Adam died? Lamech, the ninth from Adam (including Abel), and father of Noah, was fifty-six years old when Adam died.

How old was Methuselah? Two hundred and forty-three years.

How old was Enoch? Three hundred and eight years.

How old was Jared? Four hundred and seventy years.

How old was Mahalaleel? Five hundred and thirty-five years.

How old was Cainan? Six hundred and five years.

How old was Enos? Six hundred and ninety-five years.

How old was Seth? Eight hundred years. For this item of the account, see Lecture 2:38.

How many of these noted men were cotemporary with Adam? Nine.

What are their names? Abel, Seth, Enos, Cainan, Mahalaleel, Jared, Enoch, Methuselah and Lamech. (Lecture 2:39.)

How long did Seth live after Enos was born? Eight hundred and seven years. (Gen. 5:7.)

What was Seth's age when he died? Nine hundred and twelve years. (Gen. 5:8.)

How long did Enos live after Cainan was born? Eight hundred and fifteen years. (Gen. 5:10.)

What was Enos's age when he died? Nine hundred and five years. (Gen. 5:11.)

How long did Cainan live after Mahalaleel was born? Eight hundred and forty years. (Gen. 5:13.)

What was Cainan's age when he died? Nine hundred and ten years. (Gen. 5:14.)

How long did Mahalaleel live after Jared was born? Eight hundred and thirty years. (Gen. 5:16.)

What was Mahalaleel's age when he died? Eight hundred and ninety-five years. (Gen. 5:17.)

How long did Jared live after Enoch was born? Eight hundred years. (Gen. 5:19.)

What was Jared's age when he died? Nine hundred and sixty-two years. (Gen. 5:20.)

How long did Enoch walk with God after Methuselah was born? Three hundred years. (Gen. 5:22.)

What was Enoch's age when he was translated? Three hundred and sixty-five years. (Gen. 5:23.)[9]

How long did Methuselah live after Lamech was born? Seven hundred and eighty-two years. (Gen. 5:26.)

What was Methuselah's age when he died? Nine hundred and sixty-nine years. (Gen. 5:27.)

---

9. Orson Pratt, when he edited the Doctrine and Covenants in 1879, added this footnote: "According to the Old Testament. For Enoch's age, see Covenants and Commandments, Section 107:49."

How long did Lamech live after Noah was born? Five hundred and ninety-five years. (Gen. 5:30.)

What was Lamech's age when he died? Seven hundred and seventy-seven years. (Gen. 5:31.) For the account of the last item see Lecture 2:40.

In what year of the world did Adam die? In the nine hundred and thirtieth.

In what year was Enoch translated? In the nine hundred and eighty-seventh.[10]

In what year did Seth die? In the one thousand and forty-second.

In what year did Enos die? In the eleven hundred and fortieth.

In what year did Cainan die? In the twelve hundred and thirty-fifth.

In what year did Mahalaleel die? In the twelve hundred and ninetieth.

In what year did Jared die? In the fourteen hundred and twenty-second.

In what year did Lamech die? In the sixteen hundred and fifty-first.

In what year did Methuselah die? In the sixteen hundred and fifty-sixth. For this account see Lecture 2:41.

How old was Noah when Enos died? Eighty-four years.

How old when Cainan died? One hundred and seventy-nine years.

How old when Mahalaleel died? Two hundred and thirty-four years.

How old when Jared died? Three hundred and sixty-six years.

How old when Lamech died? Five hundred and ninety-five years.

How old when Methuselah died? Six hundred years. See Lecture 2:42, for the last item.

How many of those men lived in the days of Noah? Six.

---

10. Orson Pratt, when he edited the Doctrine and Covenants in 1879, added this footnote: "For Enoch's age, see Covenants and Commandments, Section 107:49."

What are their names? Enos, Cainan, Mahalaleel, Jared, Methuselah, and Lamech. (Lecture 2:43.)

How many of those men were cotemporary with Adam and Noah both? Six.

What are their names? Enos, Cainan, Mahalaleel, Jared, Methuselah, and Lamech. (Lectures 2:43.)

According to the foregoing account, how was the knowledge of the existence of God first suggested to the minds of men? By the manifestation made to our father Adam, when he was in the presence of God, both before and while he was in Eden. (Lecture 2:44.)

How was the knowledge of the existence of God disseminated among the inhabitants of the world? By tradition from father to son. (Lecture 2:44.)

How old was Noah when Shem was born? Five hundred and two years. (Gen. 5:32.)

What was the term of years from the birth of Shem to the flood? Ninety-eight.

What was the term of years that Noah lived after the flood? Three hundred and fifty. (Gen. 9:28.)

What was Noah's age when he died? Nine hundred and fifty years. (Gen. 9:29; Lecture 2:45.)

What was Shem's age when Arphaxad was born? One hundred years. (Gen. 11:10.)

What was Arphaxad's age when Salah was born? Thirty-five years. (Gen. 11:12.)

What was Salah's age when Eber was born? Thirty years. (Gen. 11:14.)

What was Eber's age when Peleg was born? Thirty-four years. (Gen. 11:16.)

What was Peleg's age when Reu was born? Thirty years. (Gen. 11:18.)

What was Reu's age when Serug was born? Thirty-two years. (Gen. 11:20.)

What was Serug's age when Nahor was born? Thirty years. (Gen. 11:22.)

What was Nahor's age when Terah was born? Twenty-nine years. (Gen. 11:24.)

What was Terah's age when Nahor (the [brother] of Abraham) was born? Seventy years. (Gen. 11:26.)

What was Terah's age when Abraham was born? Some suppose one hundred and thirty years, and others seventy. (Gen. 11:26; Lecture 2:46.)

What was the number of years from the flood to the birth of Abraham? Supposing Abraham to have been born when Terah was one hundred and thirty years old, it was three hundred and fifty-two years: but if he was born when Terah was seventy years old, it was two hundred and ninety-two years. (Lecture 2:47.)

How long did Shem live after Arphaxad was born? Five hundred years. (Gen. 11:11.)

What was Shem's age when he died? Six hundred years. (Gen. 11:11.)

What number of years did Arphaxad live after Salah was born? Four hundred and three years. (Gen. 11:13.)

What was Arphaxad's age when he died? Four hundred and thirty-eight years.

What number of years did Salah live after Eber was born? Four hundred and three years.

What was Salah's age when he died? Four hundred and thirty-three years.

What number of years did Eber live after Peleg was born? Four hundred and thirty years. (Gen. 11:17.)

What was Eber's age when he died? Four hundred and sixty-four years.

What number of years did Peleg live after Reu was born? Two hundred and nine years. (Gen. 11:19.)

What was Peleg's age when he died? Two hundred and thirty-nine years.

What number of years did Reu live after Serug was born? Two hundred and seven years. (Gen. 11:21.)

What was Reu's age when he died? Two hundred and thirty-nine years.

What number of years did Serug live after Nahor was born? Two hundred years. (Gen. 11:23.)

What was Serug's age when he died? Two hundred and thirty years.

What number of years did Nahor live after Terah was born? One hundred and nineteen years. (Gen. 11:25.)

What was Nahor's age when he died? One hundred and forty-eight years.

What number of years did Terah live after Abraham was born? Supposing Terah to have been one hundred and thirty years old when Abraham was born, he lived seventy-five years; but if Abraham was born when Terah was seventy years old, he lived one hundred and thirty-five.

What was Terah's age when he died? Two hundred and five years. (Gen. 11:32.) For this account from the birth of Arphaxad to the death of Terah, see Lecture 2:48.

In what year of the world did Peleg die? Agreeable to the foregoing chronology, he died in the nineteen hundred and ninety-sixth year of the world.

In what year of the world did Nahor die? In the nineteen hundred and ninety-seventh.

In what year of the world did Noah die? In the two thousand and sixth.

In what year of the world did Reu die? In the two thousand and twenty-sixth.

In what year of the world did Serug die? In the two thousand and forty-ninth.

In what year of the world did Terah die? In the two thousand and eighty-third.

In what year of the world did Arphaxad die? In the two thousand and ninety-sixth.

In what year of the world did Salah die? In the twenty-one hundred and twenty-sixth.

In what year of the world did Abraham die? In the twenty-one hundred and eighty-third.

In what year of the world did Eber die? In the twenty-one hundred and eighty-seventh. For this account of the year of the world in which those men died, see Lecture 2:49–50.

How old was Nahor (Abraham's brother) when Noah died? Fifty-eight years.

How old was Terah? One hundred and twenty-eight.

How old was Serug? One hundred and eighty-seven.

How old was Reu? Two hundred and nineteen.

How old was Eber? Two hundred and eighty-three.

How old was Salah? Three hundred and thirteen.

How old was Arphaxad? Three hundred and forty-eight.

How old was Shem? Four hundred and forty-eight.

For the last account see Lecture 2:51.

How old was Abraham when Reu died? Eighteen years, if he was born when Terah was one hundred and thirty years old.

What was his age when Serug and Nahor (Abraham's brother) died? Forty-one years.

What was his age when Terah died? Seventy-five years.

What was his age when Arphaxad died? Eighty-eight.

What was his age when Salah died? One hundred and eighteen years.

What was his age when Shem died? One hundred and fifty years. For this see Lecture 2:52.

How many noted characters lived from Noah to Abraham? Ten.

What are their names? Shem, Arphaxad, Salah, Eber, Peleg, Reu, Serug, Nahor, Terah, and Nahor (Abraham's bro*ther). (Lecture 2:52.)*

How many of these were cotemporary with Noah? The whole.

How many with Abraham? Eight.

What are their names? Nahor (Abraham's brother), Terah, Serug, Reu, Eber, Salah, Arphaxad, and Shem. (Lecture 2:52.)

How many were cotemporary with both Noah and Abraham? Eight.

What are their names? Shem, Arphaxad, Salah, Eber, Reu, Serug, Terah, and Nahor (Abraham's brother). (Lecture 2:52.)

Did any of these men die before Noah? They did.

Who were they? Peleg, in whose days the earth was divided, and Nahor (Abraham's grandfather). (Lecture 2:49.)

Did any one of them live longer than Abraham? There was one. (Lecture 2:50.)

Who was he? Eber, the fourth from Noah. (Lecture 2:50.)

In whose days was the earth divided? In the days of Peleg.

Where have we the account given that the earth was divided in the days of Peleg? (Gen. 10:25.)

Can you repeat the sentence? "Unto Eber were born two sons: the name of one was Peleg; for in his days was the earth divided."

What testimony have men, in the first instance, that there is a God? Human testimony, and human testimony only. (Lecture 2:56.)

What excited the ancient saints to seek diligently after a knowledge of the glory of God, his perfections and attributes? The credence they gave to the testimony of their fathers. (Lecture 2:56.)

How do men obtain a knowledge of the glory of God, his perfections and attributes? By devoting themselves to his service, through prayer and supplication incessantly strengthening their faith in him, until, like Enoch, the brother of Jared, and Moses, they obtain a manifestation of God to themselves. (Lecture 2:55.)

Is the knowledge of the existence of God a matter of mere tradition, founded upon human testimony alone, until persons receive a manifestation of God to themselves? It is.

How do you prove it? From the whole of the first and second lectures.

LECTURE THIRD

1. In the second lecture it was shown how it was that the knowledge of the existence of God came into the world, and by what means the first thoughts were suggested to the minds of men that such a Being did actually exist; and that it was by reason of the knowledge of his existence that there was a foundation laid for the exercise of faith in him, as the only Being in whom faith could center for life and salvation; for faith could not center in a Being of whose existence we have no idea, because the idea of his existence in the first instance is essential to the exercise of faith in him. Romans 10:14: "How then shall they call on him in whom they have not believed? and how shall they believe in him of whom they have not heard? and how shall they hear without a preacher?" (or one sent to tell them?) So, then, faith comes by hearing the word of God. (New Translation.)

2. Let us here observe, that three things are necessary in order that any rational and intelligent being may exercise faith in God unto life and salvation.

3. First, the idea that he actually exists.

4. Secondly, a *correct* idea of his character, perfections, and attributes.

5. Thirdly, an actual knowledge that the course of life which he is pursuing is according to his will. For without an acquaintance with these three important facts, the faith of every rational being must be imperfect and unproductive; but with this understanding it can become perfect and fruitful, abounding in righteousness, unto the praise and glory of God the Father, and the Lord Jesus Christ.

6. Having previously been made acquainted with the way the idea of his existence came into the world, as well as the fact of his existence, we shall proceed to examine his character, perfections, and attributes, in order that this class may see, not only the just grounds which they have for the exercise of faith in him for life and salvation, but the reasons that all the world, also, as far as the idea of his existence extends, may have to exercise faith in him, the Father of all living.

7. As we have been indebted to a revelation which God made of himself to his creatures, in the first instance, for the idea of his existence, so in like manner we are indebted to the revelations which he has given to us for a correct understanding of his character, perfections, and attributes; because, without the revelations which he has given to us, no man by searching could find out God. (Job 11:7–9.) 1 Corinthians 2:9–11: "But as it is written, Eye hath not seen, nor ear heard, neither have entered into the heart of man, the things which God hath prepared for them that love him. But God hath revealed them unto us by his Spirit: for the Spirit searcheth all things, yea, the deep things of God. For what man knoweth the things of a man, save the spirit of man which is in him? even so the things of God knoweth no man, but the Spirit of God."

8. Having said so much we proceed to examine the character which the revelations have given of God.

9. Moses gives us the following account in Exodus 34:6: "And the Lord passed by before him, and proclaimed, The Lord, the Lord God, merciful and gracious, longsuffering and abundant in goodness and truth." Psalms 103:6–8: "The Lord executeth righteousness and judgment for all that are oppressed. He made known his ways unto Moses, his acts unto the children of Israel. The Lord is merciful and gracious, slow to anger, and plenteous in mercy." Psalms 103:17–18: "But the mercy of the Lord is from everlasting to everlasting upon them that fear him, and his righteousness unto children's children; to such as keep his covenant, and to those that remember his commandments to do them." Psalm 90:2: "Before the mountains were brought forth, or ever thou hadst formed the earth and the world, even from everlasting to everlasting, thou art God." Hebrews 1:10–12: "And, Thou, Lord, in the beginning hast laid the foundation of the earth; and the heavens are the works of thine hands: they shall perish; but thou remainest; and they all shall wax old as doth a garment; and as a vesture shalt thou fold them up, and they shall be changed: but thou art the same, and thy years shall not fail." James 1:17: "Every good gift and every perfect gift is from above, and cometh down from the Father of lights, with whom is no variableness, neither shadow of turning." Malachi 3:6: "For I am the Lord, I change not; therefore ye sons of Jacob are not consumed."

10. Book of Commandments, chapter 2, commencing in the third line of the first paragraph:[11] "For God doth not walk in crooked paths; neither doth he turn to the right hand nor the left; neither doth he vary from that which he hath said: Therefore his paths are strait, and his course is one eternal round." Book of Commandments, chapter 37, verse 1:[12] "Listen to the voice of the Lord your God, even Alpha and Omega, the beginning and the end, whose course is one eternal round, the same today as yesterday and forever."

11. Numbers 23:19: "God is not a man, that he should lie; neither the son of man, that he should repent." 1 John 4:8: "He that

_____

11. See Doctrine and Covenants 3:2.
12. Doctrine and Covenants 35:1.

loveth not knoweth not God; for God is love." Acts 10:34–35: "Then Peter opened his mouth, and said, Of a truth I perceive that God is no respecter of persons: but in every nation he that feareth him, and worketh righteousness is accepted with him."

12. From the foregoing testimonies we learn the following things respecting the character of God:

13. First, that he was God before the world was created, and the same God that he was after it was created.

14. Secondly, that he is merciful and gracious, slow to anger, abundant in goodness, and that he was so from everlasting, and will be to everlasting.

15. Thirdly, that he changes not, neither is there variableness with him; but that he is the same from everlasting to everlasting, being the same yesterday, to-day, and for ever; and that his course is one eternal round, without variation.

16. Fourthly, that he is a God of truth and cannot lie.

17. Fifthly, that he is no respecter of persons: but in every nation he that fears God and works righteousness is accepted of him.

18. Sixthly, that he is love.

19. An acquaintance with these attributes in the divine character, is essentially necessary, in order that the faith of any rational being can center in him for life and salvation. For if he did not, in the first instance, believe him to be God, that is, the Creator and upholder of all things, he could not *center* his faith in him for life and salvation, for fear there should be greater than he who would thwart all his plans, and he, like the gods of the heathen, would be unable to fulfill his promises; but seeing he is God over all, from everlasting to everlasting, the Creator and upholder of all things, no such fear can exist in the minds of those who put their trust in him, so that in this respect their faith can be without wavering.

20. But secondly; unless he was merciful and gracious, slow to anger, long-suffering and full of goodness, such is the weakness of human nature, and so great the frailties and imperfections of men, that unless they believed that these excellencies existed in the divine character, the faith necessary to salvation could not exist; for doubt would take the place of faith, and those who know

their weakness and liability to sin would be in constant doubt of salvation if it were not for the idea which they have of the excellency of the character of God, that he is slow to anger and long-suffering, and of a forgiving disposition, and does forgive iniquity, transgression, and sin. An idea of these facts does away doubt, and makes faith exceedingly strong.

21. But it is equally as necessary that men should have the idea that he is a God who changes not, in order to have faith in him, as it is to have the idea that he is gracious and long-suffering; for without the idea of unchangeableness in the character of the Deity, doubt would take the place of faith. But with the idea that he changes not, faith lays hold upon the excellencies in his character with unshaken confidence, believing he is the same yesterday, to-day, and forever, and that his course is one eternal round.

22. And again, the idea that he is a God of truth and cannot lie, is equally as necessary to the exercise of faith in him as the idea of his unchangeableness. For without the idea that he was a God of truth and could not lie, the confidence necessary to be placed in his word in order to the exercise of faith in him could not exist. But having the idea that he is not man, that he cannot lie, it gives power to the minds of men to exercise faith in him.

23. But it is also necessary that men should have an idea that he is no respecter of persons, for with the idea of all the other excellencies in his character, and this one wanting, men could not exercise faith in him; because if he were a respecter of persons, they could not tell what their privileges were, nor how far they were authorized to exercise faith in him, or whether they were authorized to do it at all, but all must be confusion; but no sooner are the minds of men made acquainted with the truth on this point, that he is no respecter of persons, than they see that they have authority by faith to lay hold on eternal life, the richest boon of heaven, because God is no respecter of persons, and that every man in every nation has an equal privilege.

24. And lastly, but not less important to the exercise of faith in God, is the idea that he is love; for with all the other excellencies in his character, without this one to influence them, they could

not have such powerful dominion over the minds of men; but when the idea is planted in the mind that he is love, who cannot see the just ground that men of every nation, kindred, and tongue, have to exercise faith in God so as to obtain eternal life?

25. From the above description of the character of the Deity, which is given him in the revelations to men, there is a sure foundation for the exercise of faith in him among every people, nation, and kindred, from age to age, and from generation to generation.

26. Let us here observe that the foregoing is the character which is given of God in his revelations to the Former-day Saints, and it is also the character which is given of him in his revelations to the Latter-day Saints, so that the saints of former days and those of latter days are both alike in this respect; the Latter-day Saints having as good grounds to exercise faith in God as the Former-day Saints had, because the same character is given of him to both.

Questions and Answers on the Foregoing Principles

What was shown in the second lecture? It was shown how the knowledge of the existence of God came into the world. (Lecture 3:1.)

What is the effect of the idea of his existence among men? It lays the foundation for the exercise of faith in him. (Lecture 3:1.)

Is the idea of his existence, in the first instance, necessary in order for the exercise of faith in him? It is. (Lecture 3:1.)

How do you prove it? By the tenth chapter of Romans and fourteenth verse. (Lecture 3:1.)

How many things are necessary for us to understand, respecting the Deity and our relation to him, in order that we may exercise faith in him for life and salvation? Three. (Lecture 3:2.)

What are they? First, that God does actually exist; secondly, correct ideas of his character, his perfections and attributes; and thirdly, that the course which we pursue is according to his mind and will. (Lecture 3:3–5.)

Would the idea of any one or two of the above-mentioned things enable a person to exercise faith in God? It would not, for without the idea of them all faith would be imperfect and unproductive. (Lecture 3:5.)

Would an idea of these three things lay a sure foundation for the exercise of faith in God, so as to obtain life and salvation? It would; for by the idea of these three things, faith could become perfect and fruitful, abounding in righteousness unto the praise and glory of God. (Lecture 3:5.)

How are we to be made acquainted with the before-mentioned things respecting the Deity, and respecting ourselves? By revelation. (Lecture 3:6.)

Could these things be found out by any other means than by revelation? They could not.

How do you prove it? By the scriptures. (Job 11:7–9; 1 Corinthians 2:9–11; Lecture 3:7.)

What things do we learn in the revelations of God respecting his character? We learn the six following things: First, that he was God before the world was created, and the same God that he was after it was created. Secondly, that he is merciful and gracious, slow to anger, abundant in goodness, and that he was so from everlasting, and will be so to everlasting. Thirdly, that he changes not, neither is there variableness with him, and that his course is one eternal round. Fourthly, that he is a God of truth, and cannot lie. Fifthly, that he is no respecter of persons; and sixthly, that he is love. (Lecture 3:12–18.)

Where do you find the revelations which give us this idea of the character of the Deity? In the bible and book of commandments, and they are quoted in the third lecture. (Lecture 3:9–11.)

What effect would it have on any rational being not to have an idea that the Lord was God, the Creator and upholder of all things? It would prevent him from exercising faith in him unto life and salvation.

Why would it prevent him from exercising faith in God? Because he would be as the heathen, not knowing but there might be a being greater and more powerful than he, and thereby he be prevented from fulfilling his promises. (Lecture 3:19.)

Does this idea prevent this doubt? It does; for persons having this idea are enabled thereby to exercise faith without this doubt. (Lecture 3:19.)

Is it not also necessary to have the idea that God is merciful and gracious, long-suffering and full of goodness? It is. (Lecture 3:20.)

Why is it necessary? Because of the weakness and imperfections of human nature, and the great frailties of man; for such is the weakness of man, and such his frailties, that he is liable to sin continually, and if God were not long-suffering, and full of compassion, gracious and merciful, and of a forgiving disposition, man would be cut off from before him, in consequence of which he would be in continual doubt and could not exercise faith; for where doubt is, there faith has no power; but by man's believing that God is full of compassion and forgiveness, long-suffering and slow to anger, he can exercise faith in him and overcome doubt, so as to be exceedingly strong. (Lecture 3:20.)

Is it not equally as necessary that man should have an idea that God changes not, neither is there variableness with him, in order to exercise faith in him unto life and salvation? It is; because without this, he would not know how soon the mercy of God might change into cruelty, his long-suffering into rashness, his love into hatred, and in consequence of which doubt man would be incapable of exercising faith in him, but having the idea that he is unchangeable, man can have faith in him continually, believing that what he was yesterday he is to-day, and will be forever. (Lecture 3:21.)

Is it not necessary also, for men to have an idea that God is a being of truth before they can have perfect faith in him? It is; for unless men have this idea they cannot place confidence in his word, and, not being able to place confidence in his word, they could not have faith in him; but believing that he is a God of truth, and that his word cannot fail, their faith can rest in him without doubt. (Lecture 3:22.)

Could man exercise faith in God so as to obtain eternal life unless he believed that God was no respecter of persons? He could not; because without this idea he could not certainly know that it was his privilege so to do, and in consequence of this doubt his faith could not be sufficiently strong to save him. (Lecture 3:23.)

Would it be possible for a man to exercise faith in God, so as to be saved, unless he had an idea that God was love? He could not; because man could not love God unless he had an idea that God was love, and if he did not love God he could not have faith in him. (Lecture 3:24.)

What is the description which the sacred writers give of the character of the Deity calculated to do? It is calculated to lay a foundation for the exercise of faith in him, as far as the knowledge extends, among all people, tongues, languages, kindreds and nations, and that from age to age, and from generation to generation. (Lecture 3:25.)

Is the character which God has given of himself uniform? It is, in all his revelations, whether to the Former-day Saints, or to the Latter-day Saints, so that they all have the authority to exercise faith in him, and to expect, by the exercise of their faith, to enjoy the same blessings. (Lecture 3:26.)

LECTURE FOURTH

1. Having shown, in the third lecture, that correct ideas of the character of God are necessary in order to the exercise of faith in him unto life and salvation; and that without correct ideas of his character the minds of men could not have sufficient power with God to the exercise of faith necessary to the enjoyment of eternal life; and that correct ideas of his character lay a foundation, as far as his character is concerned, for the exercise of faith, so as to enjoy the fullness of the blessing of the gospel of Jesus Christ, even that of eternal glory; we shall now proceed to show the connection there is between correct ideas of the attributes of God, and the exercise of faith in him unto eternal life.

2. Let us here observe, that the real design which the God of heaven had in view in making the human family acquainted with his attributes, was, that they, through the ideas of the existence of his attributes, might be enabled to exercise faith in him, and, through the exercise of faith in him, might obtain eternal life; for without the idea of the existence of the attributes which belong to God the minds of men could not have power to exercise faith in him so as to lay hold upon eternal life. The God of heaven, understanding most perfectly the constitution of human nature, and the weakness of men, knew what was necessary to

be revealed, and what ideas must be planted in their minds in order that they might be enabled to exercise faith in him unto eternal life.

3. Having said so much, we shall proceed to examine the attributes of God, as set forth in his revelations to the human family and to show how necessary correct ideas of his attributes are to enable men to exercise faith in him; for without these ideas being planted in the minds of men it would be out of the power of any person or persons to exercise faith in God so as to obtain eternal life. So that the divine communications made to men in the first instance were designed to establish in their minds the ideas necessary to enable them to exercise faith in God, and through this means to be partakers of his glory.

4. We have, in the revelations which he has given to the human family, the following account of his attributes:

5. First—Knowledge. Acts 15:18: "Known unto God are all his works from the beginning of the world." Isaiah 46:9–10 (italics added): "Remember the former things of old: for I am God, and there is none else; I am God, and there is none like me, *declaring the end from the beginning,* and from ancient times the things that are not yet done, saying, My counsel shall stand, and I will do all my pleasure."

6. Secondly—Faith or power. Hebrews 11:3: "Through faith we understand that the worlds were framed by the word of God." Genesis 1:1: "In the beginning God created the heaven and the earth." Isaiah 14:24, 27: "The Lord of hosts hath sworn, saying, Surely as I have thought, so shall it come to pass; and as I have purposed, so shall it stand. . . . For the Lord of hosts hath purposed, and who shall disannul it? and his hand is stretched out, and who shall turn it back?"

7. Thirdly—Justice. Psalm 89:14: "Justice and judgment are the habitation of thy throne." Isaiah 45:21: "Tell ye, and bring them near; yea, let them take counsel together: who hath declared this from ancient time? . . . have not I the Lord? and there is no God else beside me; a just God and a Saviour." Zephaniah 3:5: "The just Lord is in the midst thereof." Zechariah 9:9: "Rejoice greatly, O daughter of Zion; shout, O daughter of Jerusa-

lem: behold, thy King cometh unto thee: he is just, and having salvation."

8. Fourthly—Judgment. Psalm 89:14: "Justice and judgment are the habitation of thy throne." Deuteronomy 32:4: "He is the Rock, his work is perfect: for all his ways are judgment: a God of truth and without iniquity, just and right is he." Psalm 9:7: "But the Lord shall endure for ever: he hath prepared his throne for judgment." Psalm 9:16: "The Lord is known by the judgment which he executeth."

9. Fifthly—Mercy. Psalm 89:14: "Mercy and truth shall go before thy face." Exodus 34:6: "And the Lord passed by before him, and proclaimed, The Lord, the Lord God, merciful and gracious." Nehemiah 9:17: "But thou art a God ready to pardon, gracious and merciful."

10. And sixthly—Truth. Psalm 89:14: "Mercy and truth shall go before thy face." Exodus 34:6: "Long-suffering; and abundant in goodness and truth." Deuteronomy 32:4: "He is the Rock, his work is perfect: for all his ways are judgment: a God of truth and without iniquity, just and right is he." Psalm 31:5: "Into thine hand I commit my spirit: thou hast redeemed me, O Lord God of truth."

11. By a little reflection it will be seen that the idea of the existence of these attributes in the Deity is necessary to enable any rational being to exercise faith in him; for without the idea of the existence of these attributes in the Deity men could not exercise faith in him for life and salvation; seeing that without the knowledge of all things God would not be able to save any portion of his creatures; for it is by reason of the knowledge which he has of all things, from the beginning to the end, that enables him to give that understanding to his creatures by which they are made partakers of eternal life; and if it were not for the idea existing in the minds of men that God had all knowledge it would be impossible for them to exercise faith in him.

12. And it is not less necessary that men should have the idea of the existence of the attribute power in the Deity; for unless God had power over all things, and was able by his power to control all things, and thereby deliver his creatures who put their

trust in him from the power of all beings that might seek their destruction, whether in heaven, on earth, or in hell, men could not be saved. But with the idea of the existence of this attribute planted in the mind, men feel as though they had nothing to fear who put their trust in God, believing that he has power to save all who come to him to the very uttermost.

13. It is also necessary, in order to the exercise of faith in God unto life and salvation, that men should have the idea of the existence of the attribute justice in him; for without the idea of the existence of the attribute justice in the Deity men could not have confidence sufficient to place themselves under his guidance and direction; for they would be filled with fear and doubt lest the judge of all the earth would not do right, and thus fear or doubt, existing in the mind, would preclude the possibility of the exercise of faith in him for life and salvation. But when the idea of the existence of the attribute justice in the Deity is fairly planted in the mind, it leaves no room for doubt to get into the heart, and the mind is enabled to cast itself upon the Almighty without fear and without doubt, and with the most unshaken confidence, believing that the Judge of all the earth will do right.

14. It is also of equal importance that men should have the idea of the existence of the attribute judgment in God, in order that they may exercise faith in him for life and salvation; for without the idea of the existence of this attribute in the Deity, it would be impossible for men to exercise faith in him for life and salvation, seeing that it is through the exercise of this attribute that the faithful in Christ Jesus are delivered out of the hands of those who seek their destruction; for if God were not to come out in swift judgment against the workers of iniquity and the powers of darkness, his saints could not be saved; for it is by judgment that the Lord delivers his saints out of the hands of all their enemies, and those who reject the gospel of our Lord Jesus Christ. But no sooner is the idea of the existence of this attribute planted in the minds of men, than it gives power to the mind for the exercise of faith and confidence in God, and they are enabled by faith to lay hold on the promises which are set before them, and wade through all the tribulations and afflictions

to which they are subjected by reason of the persecution from those who know not God, and obey not the gospel of our Lord Jesus Christ, believing that in due time the Lord will come out in swift judgment against their enemies, and they shall be cut off from before him, and that in his own due time he will bear them off conquerors, and more than conquerors, in all things.

15. And again, it is equally important that men should have the idea of the existence of the attribute mercy in the Deity, in order to exercise faith in him for life and salvation; for without the idea of the existence of this attribute in the Deity, the spirits of the saints would faint in the midst of the tribulations, afflictions, and persecutions which they have to endure for righteousness' sake. But when the idea of the existence of this attribute is once established in the mind it gives life and energy to the spirits of the saints, believing that the mercy of God will be poured out upon them in the midst of their afflictions, and that he will compassionate them in their sufferings, and that the mercy of God will lay hold of them and secure them in the arms of his love, so that they will receive a full reward for all their sufferings.

16. And lastly, but not less important to the exercise of faith in God, is the idea of the existence of the attribute truth in him; for without the idea of the existence of this attribute the mind of man could have nothing upon which it could rest with certainty—all would be confusion and doubt. But with the idea of the existence of this attribute in the Deity in the mind, all the teachings, instructions, promises, and blessings, become realities, and the mind is enabled to lay hold of them with certainty and confidence, believing that these things, and all that the Lord has said, shall be fulfilled in their time; and that all the cursings, denunciations, and judgments, pronounced upon the heads of the unrighteous, will also be executed in the due time of the Lord: and, by reason of the truth and veracity of him, the mind beholds its deliverance and salvation as being certain.

17. Let the mind once reflect sincerely and candidly upon the ideas of the existence of the before-mentioned attributes in the Deity, and it will be seen that, as far as his attributes are concerned, there is a sure foundation laid for the exercise of faith in

him for life and salvation. For inasmuch as God possesses the attribute knowledge, he can make all things known to his saints necessary for their salvation; and as he possesses the attribute power, he is able thereby to deliver them from the power of all enemies; and seeing, also, that justice is an attribute of the Deity, he will deal with them upon the principles of righteousness and equity, and a just reward will be granted unto them for all their afflictions and sufferings for the truth's sake. And as judgment is an attribute of the Deity also, his saints can have the most unshaken confidence that they will, in due time, obtain a perfect deliverance out of the hands of all their enemies, and a complete victory over all those who have sought their hurt and destruction. And as mercy is also an attribute of the Deity, his saints can have confidence that it will be exercised towards them, and through the exercise of that attribute towards them comfort and consolation will be administered unto them abundantly, amid all their afflictions and tribulations. And, lastly, realizing that truth is an attribute of the Deity, the mind is led to rejoice amid all its trials and temptations, in hope of that glory which is to be brought at the revelation of Jesus Christ, and in view of that crown which is to be placed upon the heads of the saints in the day when the Lord shall distribute rewards unto them, and in prospect of that eternal weight of glory which the Lord has promised to bestow upon them, when he shall bring them in the midst of his throne to dwell in his presence eternally.

18. In view, then, of the existence of these attributes, the faith of the saints can become exceedingly strong, abounding in righteousness unto the praise and glory of God, and can exert its mighty influence in searching after wisdom and understanding, until it has obtained a knowledge of all things that pertain to life and salvation.

19. Such, then, is the foundation which is laid, through the revelation of the attributes of God, for the exercise of faith in him for life and salvation; and seeing that these are attributes of the Deity, they are unchangeable—being the same yesterday, to-day, and for ever—which gives to the minds of the Latter-day Saints the same power and authority to exercise faith in God which

the Former-day Saints had; so that all the saints, in this respect, have been, are, and will be, alike until the end of time; for God never changes, therefore his attributes and character remain forever the same. And as it is through the revelation of these that a foundation is laid for the exercise of faith in God unto life and salvation, the foundation, therefore, for the exercise of faith was, is, and ever will be, the same; so that all men have had, and will have, an equal privilege.

Questions and Answers on the Foregoing Principles

What was shown in the third lecture? It was shown that correct ideas of the character of God are necessary in order to exercise faith in him unto life and salvation; and that without correct ideas of his character, men could not have power to exercise faith in him unto life and salvation, but that correct ideas of his character, as far as his character was concerned in the exercise of faith in him, lay a sure foundation for the exercise of it. (Lecture 4:1.)

What object had the God of Heaven in revealing his attributes to men? That through an acquaintance with his attributes they might be enabled to exercise faith in him so as to obtain eternal life. (Lecture 4:2.)

Could men exercise faith in God without an acquaintance with his attributes, so as to be enabled to lay hold of eternal life? They could not. (Lecture 4:2–3.)

What account is given of the attributes of God in his revelations? First, Knowledge; secondly, Faith or Power; thirdly, Justice; fourthly, Judgment; fifthly, Mercy; and sixthly, Truth. (Lecture 4:4–10.)

Where are the revelations to be found which give this relation of the attributes of God? In the Old and New Testaments, and they are quoted in the fourth lecture, fifth, sixth, seventh, eighth, ninth and tenth paragraphs. [Let the student turn and commit these paragraphs to memory.]

Is the idea of the existence of these attributes in the Deity necessary in order to enable any rational being to exercise faith in him unto life and salvation? It is.

How do you prove it? By the eleventh, twelfth, thirteenth, fourteenth, fifteenth and sixteenth paragraphs in this lecture. [Let the student turn and commit these paragraphs to memory.]

Does the idea of the existence of these attributes in the Deity, as far as his attributes are concerned, enable a rational being to exercise faith in him unto life and salvation? It does. How do you prove it? By the seventeenth and eighteenth paragraphs. [Let the student turn and commit these paragraphs to memory.]

Have the Latter-day Saints as much authority given them, through the revelation of the attributes of God, to exercise faith in him as the Former-day Saints had? They have.

How do you prove it? By the nineteenth paragraph of this lecture. [Let the student turn and commit this paragraph to memory.]

LECTURE FIFTH

1. In our former lectures we treated of the being, character, perfections, and attributes, of God. What we mean by perfections is, the perfections which belong to all the attributes of his nature. We shall, in this lecture, speak of the Godhead—we mean the Father, Son, and Holy Spirit.

2. There are two personages who constitute the great, matchless, governing, and supreme, power over all things, by whom all things were created and made, that are created and made, whether visible or invisible, whether in heaven, on earth, or in the earth, under the earth, or throughout the immensity of space. They are the Father and the Son—the Father being a personage of spirit,[13] glory, and power, possessing all perfection and fullness, the Son, who was in the bosom of the Father, a personage of tabernacle, made or fashioned like unto man, or being in the form and likeness of man, or rather man was formed after his

---

13. At this point in Church history, the Prophet and his associates may not have understood what was later revealed in D&C 130:22: "The Father has a body of flesh and bones as tangible as man's; the Son also; but the Holy Ghost has not a body of flesh and bones, but is a personage of Spirit."

likeness and in his image; he is also the express image and likeness of the personage of the Father, possessing all the fullness of the Father, or the same fullness with the Father; being begotten of him, and ordained from before the foundation of the world to be a propitiation for the sins of all those who should believe on his name, and is called the Son because of the flesh, and descended in suffering below that which man can suffer; or, in other words, suffered greater sufferings, and was exposed to more powerful contradictions than any man can be. But, notwithstanding all this, he kept the law of God, and remained without sin, showing thereby that it is in the power of man to keep the law and remain also without sin; and also, that by him a righteous judgment might come upon all flesh, and that all who walk not in the law of God may justly be condemned by the law, and have no excuse for their sins. And he being the Only Begotten of the Father, full of grace and truth, and having overcome, received a fullness of the glory of the Father, possessing the same mind with the Father, which mind is the Holy Spirit,[14] that bears record of the Father and the Son, and these three are one; or, in other words, these three constitute the great, matchless, governing and supreme, power over all things; by whom all things were created and made that were created and made, and these three constitute the Godhead, and are one; the Father and the Son possessing the same mind, the same wisdom, glory, power, and fullness—filling all in all; the Son being filled with the fullness of the mind, glory, and power; or, in other words, the spirit, glory, and power, of the Father, possessing all knowledge and glory, and the same kingdom, sitting at the right hand of power, in the express image and likeness of the Father, mediator for man, being filled with the fullness of the mind of the Father; or, in other words, the Spirit

---

14. This is not necessarily saying that the Holy Spirit is not a personage; it could instead refer to his role in the Godhead. As Paul wrote: "The natural man receiveth not the things of the Spirit of God: for they are foolishness unto him: neither can he know them, because they are spiritually discerned. But he that is spiritual judgeth all things, yet he himself is judged of no man. For who hath known the mind of the Lord, that he may instruct him? But we have the mind of Christ [meaning the Holy Ghost]." (1 Corinthians 9–16.)

of the Father, which Spirit is shed forth upon all who believe on his name and keep his commandments; and all those who keep his commandments shall grow up from grace to grace, and become heirs of the heavenly kingdom, and joint heirs with Jesus Christ; possessing the same mind, being transformed into the same image or likeness, even the express image of him who fills all in all; being filled with the fullness of his glory, and become one in him, even as the Father, Son and Holy Spirit are one.

3. From the foregoing account of the Godhead, which is given in his revelations, the saints have a sure foundation laid for the exercise of faith unto life and salvation, through the atonement and mediation of Jesus Christ; by whose blood they have a forgiveness of sins, and also a sure reward laid up for them in heaven, even that of partaking of the fullness of the Father and the Son through the Spirit. As the Son partakes of the fullness of the Father through the Spirit, so the saints are, by the same Spirit, to be partakers of the same fullness, to enjoy the same glory; for as the Father and the Son are one, so, in like manner, the saints are to be one in them. Through the love of the Father, the mediation of Jesus Christ, and the gift of the Holy Spirit, they are to be heirs of God, and joint heirs with Jesus Christ.

Questions and Answers on the Foregoing Principles

Of what do the foregoing lectures treat? Of the being, perfections, and attributes of the Deity. (Lecture 5:1.)

What are we to understand by the perfections of the Deity? The perfections which belong to his attributes.

How many personages are there in the Godhead? Two: the Father and Son. (Lecture 5:1.)[15]

How do you prove that there are two personages in the Godhead? By the Scriptures. Genesis 1:26; also Lecture 2:6:[16] "And I, God,

---

15. Actually, the referenced paragraph says there are three, including the Holy Spirit. Paragraph 2 says "these three [Father, Son, and Holy Spirit] constitute the Godhead."

16. See Joseph Smith Translation, Genesis 1:27; Moses 2:26.

said unto mine Only Begotten, which was with me from the beginning, Let us make man in our image, after our likeness; and
it was so." Genesis 3:22:[17] "And I, the Lord God, said unto mine
Only Begotten, Behold, the man is become as one of us, to know
good and evil." John 17:5: "And now, O Father, glorify thou me
with thine own self with the glory which I had with thee before
the world was." (Lecture 5:2.)

What is the Father? He is a personage of glory and of power.
(Lecture 5:2.)

*How do you prove that the Father is a personage of glory and of
power?* Isaiah 60:19: "The sun shall be no more thy light by day;
neither for brightness shall the moon give light unto thee: but
the Lord shall be unto thee an everlasting light, and thy God thy
glory." 1 Chronicles 29:11: "Thine, O Lord, is the greatness, and
the power, and the glory." Psalm 29:3: "The voice of the Lord
is upon the waters: the God of glory thundereth." Psalm 79:9:
"Help us, O God of our salvation, for the glory of thy name."
Romans 1:23: "And changed the glory of the uncorruptible God
into an image made like to corruptible man." Secondly, of power.
1 Chronicles 29:11: "Thine, O Lord, is the greatness, and the
power, and the glory." Jeremiah 32:17: "Ah Lord God! behold,
thou hast made the heaven and the earth by thy great power
and stretched out arm, and there is nothing too hard for thee."
Deuteronomy 4:37: "And because he loved thy fathers, therefore
he chose their seed after them, and brought thee out in his sight
with his mighty power." 2 Samuel 22:33: "God is my strength
and power." Job 26, commencing with the 7th verse to the end of
the chapter: "He stretcheth out the north over the empty place,
and hangeth the earth upon nothing. He bindeth up the waters
in his thick clouds; and the cloud is not rent under them. He
holdeth back the face of his throne, and spreadeth his cloud
upon it. He hath compassed the waters with bounds, until the
day and night come to an end. The pillars of heaven tremble and
are astonished at his reproof. He divideth the sea with his power,
and by his understanding he smiteth through the proud. By his

17. Joseph Smith Translation, Genesis 3:28; Moses 4:28.

spirit he hath garnished the heavens; his hand hath formed the crooked serpent. Lo, these are parts of his ways: but how little a portion is heard of him? but the thunder of his power who can understand?"

What is the Son? First, he is a personage of tabernacle. (Lecture 5:2.)

How do you prove it? John 14:9–11: "Jesus saith unto him, Have I been so long time with you, and yet hast thou not known me, Philip? he that hath seen me hath seen the Father; and how sayest thou then, Shew us the Father? Believest thou not that I am in the Father, and the Father in me? the words that I speak unto you I speak not of myself: but the Father that dwelleth in me, he doeth the works. Believe me that I am in the Father, and the Father in me." Secondly, and being a personage of tabernacle, was made or fashioned like unto man, or being in the form and likeness of man. (Lecture 5:2.) Philippians 2:5–8: "Let this mind be in you, which was also in Christ Jesus: who, being in the form of God, thought it not robbery to be equal with God: but made himself of no reputation, and took upon him the form of a servant, and was made in the likeness of men: and being found in fashion as a man, he humbled himself, and became obedient unto death, even the death of the cross." Hebrews 2:14, 16: "Forasmuch then as the children are partakers of flesh and blood, he also himself likewise took part of the same. . . . For verily he took not on him the nature of angels; but he took on him the seed of Abraham." Thirdly, he is also in the likeness of the personage of the Father. (Lecture 5:2.) Hebrews 1:1–3: "God, who at sundry times and in divers manners spake in time past unto the fathers by the prophets, hath in these last days spoken unto us by his Son, whom he hath appointed heir of all things, by whom also he made the worlds; who being the brightness of his glory, and the express image of his person." Again, Philippians 2:5–6: "Let this mind be in you, which was also in Christ Jesus: who, being in the form of God, thought it not robbery to be equal with God."

Was it by the Father and the Son that all things were created and made that were created and made? It was. Colossians 1:15–17: "Who is the image of the invisible God, the firstborn of every creature:

for by him were all things created, that are in heaven, and that are in earth, visible and invisible, whether they be thrones, or dominions, or principalities, or powers: all things were created by him, and for him: and he is before all things, and by him all things consist." Genesis 1:1: "In the beginning God created the heaven and the earth." Hebrews 1:2: [God] "hath in these last days spoken unto us by his Son, whom he hath appointed heir of all things, by whom also he made the worlds."

Does he possess the fullness of the Father? He does. Colossians 1:19; 2:9: "For it pleased the Father that in him should all fulness dwell." "For in him dwelleth all the fulness of the Godhead bodily." Ephesians 1:23: "Which is his [Christ's] body, the fulness of him that filleth all in all."

Why was he called the Son? Because of the flesh. Luke 1:35: "That holy thing which shall be born of thee, shall be called the Son of God." Matthew 3:16–17: "And Jesus, when he was baptized, went up straightway out of the water, and, lo, the heavens were opened unto him, and he [John] saw the Spirit of God descending like a dove, and lighting upon him: and lo a voice from heaven, saying, This is my beloved Son, in whom I am well pleased."[18]

Was he ordained of the Father, from before the foundation of the world, to be a propitiation for the sins of all those who should believe on his name? He was. 1 Peter 1:18–20: "Forasmuch as ye know that ye were not redeemed with corruptible things, as silver and gold, from your vain conversation received by tradition from your fathers; but with the precious blood of Christ, as of a lamb without blemish and without spot: who verily was foreordained before the foundation of the world, but was manifest in these last times for you." Revelation 13:8: "And all that dwell upon the earth shall worship him [the beast], whose names are not written in the book of life of the Lamb slain from the foundation of the world." 1 Corinthians 2:7: "But we speak the wisdom of God in a mystery, even the hidden wisdom, which God ordained before the world unto our glory."

---

18. Joseph Smith Translation, Matthew 3:45–46.

Do the Father and the Son possess the same mind? They do. John 5:30: "I [Christ] can of mine own self do nothing: as I hear, I judge: and my judgment is just; because I seek not mine own will, but the will of the Father which hath sent me." John 6:38: "For I [Christ] came down from heaven, not to do mine own will, but the will of him that sent me." John 10:30: "I [Christ] and my Father are one."

What is this mind? The Holy Spirit. John 15:26: "But when the Comforter is come, whom I will send unto you from the Father, even the Spirit of truth, which proceedeth from the Father, he shall testify of me [Christ]." Galatians 4:6: "And because ye are sons, God hath sent forth the Spirit of his Son into your hearts."

Do the Father, Son, and Holy Spirit constitute the Godhead? They do. (Lecture 5:2.) [Let the student turn and commit this paragraph to memory.]

Do the believers in Christ Jesus, through the gift of the Spirit, become one with the Father and the Son, as the Father and the Son are one? They do. John 17:20–21: "Neither pray I for these [the apostles] alone, but for them also which shall believe on me through their word; that they all may be one; as thou, Father, art in me, and I in thee, that they also may be one in us: that the world may believe that thou hast sent me."

Does the foregoing account of the Godhead lay a sure foundation for the exercise of faith in him unto life and salvation? It does.

How do you prove it? By the third paragraph of this lecture. [Let the student turn and commit this paragraph to memory.]

LECTURE SIXTH

1. Having treated in the preceding lectures of the ideas, of the character, perfections, and attributes of God, we next proceed to treat of the knowledge which persons must have, that the course of life which they pursue is according to the will of God, in order that they may be enabled to exercise faith in him unto life and salvation.

2. This knowledge supplies an important place in revealed religion; for it was by reason of it that the ancients were enabled to

endure as seeing him who is invisible. An actual knowledge to any person, that the course of life which he pursues is according to the will of God, is essentially necessary to enable him to have that confidence in God without which no person can obtain eternal life. It was this that enabled the ancient saints to endure all their afflictions and persecutions, and to take joyfully the spoiling of their goods, knowing (not believing merely) that they had a more enduring substance. (Heb. 10:34.)

3. Having the assurance that they were pursuing a course which was agreeable to the will of God, they were enabled to take, not only the spoiling of their goods, and the wasting of their substance, joyfully, but also to suffer death in its most horrid forms; knowing (not merely believing) that when this earthly house of their tabernacle was dissolved, they had a building of God, a house not made with hands, eternal in the heavens. (2 Cor. 5:1.)

4. Such was, and always will be, the situation of the saints of God, that unless they have an actual knowledge that the course they are pursuing is according to the will of God they will grow weary in their minds, and faint; for such has been, and always will be, the opposition in the hearts of unbelievers and those that know not God against the pure and unadulterated religion of heaven (the only thing which insures eternal life), that they will persecute to the uttermost all that worship God according to his revelations, receive the truth in the love of it, and submit themselves to be guided and directed by his will; and drive them to such extremities that nothing short of an actual knowledge of their being the favorites of heaven, and of their having embraced that order of things which God has established for the redemption of man, will enable them to exercise that confidence in him, necessary for them to overcome the world, and obtain that crown of glory which is laid up for them that fear God.

5. For a man to lay down his all, his character and reputation, his honor, and applause, his good name among men, his houses, his lands, his brothers and sisters, his wife and children, and even his own life also—counting all things but filth and dross for the excellency of the knowledge of Jesus Christ—requires more

than mere belief or supposition that he is doing the will of God; but actual knowledge, realizing that, when these sufferings are ended, he will enter into eternal rest, and be a partaker of the glory of God.

6. For unless a person does know that he is walking according to the will of God, it would be offering an insult to the dignity of the Creator were he to say that he would be a partaker of his glory when he should be done with the things of this life. But when he has this knowledge, and most assuredly knows that he is doing the will of God, his confidence can be equally strong that he will be a partaker of the glory of God.

7. Let us here observe, that a religion that does not require the sacrifice of all things never has power sufficient to produce the faith necessary unto life and salvation; for, from the first existence of man, the faith necessary unto the enjoyment of life and salvation never could be obtained without the sacrifice of all earthly things. It was through this sacrifice, and this only, that God has ordained that men should enjoy eternal life; and it is through the medium of the sacrifice of all earthly things that men do actually know that they are doing the things that are well pleasing in the sight of God. When a man has offered in sacrifice all that he has for the truth's sake, not even withholding his life, and believing before God that he has been called to make this sacrifice because he seeks to do his will, he does know, most assuredly, that God does and will accept his sacrifice and offering, and that he has not, nor will not seek his face in vain. Under these circumstances, then, he can obtain the faith necessary for him to lay hold on eternal life.

8. It is in vain for persons to fancy to themselves that they are heirs with those, or can be heirs with them, who have offered their all in sacrifice, and by this means obtained faith in God and favor with him so as to obtain eternal life, unless they, in like manner, offer unto him the same sacrifice, and through that offering obtain the knowledge that they are accepted of him.

9. It was in offering sacrifices that Abel, the first martyr, obtained knowledge that he was accepted of God. And from the days of righteous Abel to the present time, the knowledge that

men have that they are accepted in the sight of God is obtained by offering sacrifice. And in the last days, before the Lord comes, he is to gather together his saints who have made a covenant with him by sacrifice. Psalms 50:3–5: "Our God shall come, and shall not keep silence: a fire shall devour before him, and it shall be very tempestuous round about him. He shall call to the heavens from above, and to the earth, that he may judge his people. Gather my saints together unto me; those that have made a covenant with me by sacrifice."

10. Those, then, who make the sacrifice, will have the testimony that their course is pleasing in the sight of God; and those who have this testimony will have faith to lay hold on eternal life, and will be enabled, through faith, to endure unto the end, and receive the crown that is laid up for them that love the appearing of our Lord Jesus Christ. But those who do not make the sacrifice cannot enjoy this faith, because men are dependent upon this sacrifice in order to obtain this faith: therefore, they cannot lay hold upon eternal life, because the revelations of God do not guarantee unto them the authority so to do, and without this guarantee faith could not exist.

11. All the saints of whom we have account, in all the revelations of God which are extant, obtained the knowledge which they had of their acceptance in his sight through the sacrifice which they offered unto him; and through the knowledge thus obtained their faith became sufficiently strong to lay hold upon the promise of eternal life, and to endure as seeing him who is invisible; and were enabled, through faith, to combat the powers of darkness, contend against the wiles of the adversary, overcome the world, and obtain the end of their faith, even the salvation of their souls.

12. But those who have not made this sacrifice to God do not know that the course which they pursue is well pleasing in his sight; for whatever may be their belief or their opinion, it is a matter of doubt and uncertainty in their mind; and where doubt and uncertainty are there faith is not, nor can it be. For doubt and faith do not exist in the same person at the same time; so that persons whose minds are under doubts and fears cannot

have unshaken confidence; and where unshaken confidence is not there faith is weak; and where faith is weak the persons will not be able to contend against all the opposition, tribulations, and afflictions which they will have to encounter in order to be heirs of God, and joint heirs with Christ Jesus; and they will grow weary in their minds, and the adversary will have power over them and destroy them.

[This lecture is so plain, and the facts set forth so self-evident that it is deemed unnecessary to form a catechism upon it; the student is, therefore, instructed to commit the whole to memory.]

LECTURE SEVENTH

1. In the preceding lessons we treated of what faith was, and of the object on which it rested. Agreeable to our plan, we now proceed to speak of its effects.

2. As we have seen in our former lectures that faith was the principle of action and of power in all intelligent beings, both in heaven and on earth, it will not be expected that we shall, in a lecture of this description, attempt to unfold all its effects; neither is it necessary to our purpose so to do, for it would embrace all things in heaven and on earth, and encompass all the creations of God, with all their endless varieties; for no world has yet been framed that was not framed by faith, neither has there been an intelligent being on any of God's creations who did not get there by reason of faith as it existed in himself or in some other being; nor has there been a change or a revolution in any of the creations of God, but it has been effected by faith; neither will there be a change or a revolution, unless it is effected in the same way, in any of the vast creations of the Almighty, for it is by faith that the Deity works.

3. Let us here offer some explanation in relation to faith, that our meaning may be clearly comprehended. We ask, then, what are we to understand by a man's working by faith? We answer— we understand that when a man works by faith he works by mental exertion instead of physical force. It is by words, instead of exerting his physical powers, with which every being works

when he works by faith. God said, "Let there be light: and there was light." Joshua spake, and the great lights which God had created stood still. Elijah commanded, and the heavens were stayed for the space of three years and six months, so that it did not rain: he again commanded and the heavens gave forth rain. All this was done by faith. And the Saviour says, "If you have faith as a grain of mustard seed, say to this mountain, 'Remove,' and it will remove; or say to that sycamine tree, 'Be ye plucked up, and planted in the midst of the sea,' and it shall obey you."[19] Faith, then, works by words; and with these its mightiest works have been, and will be, performed.

4. It surely will not be required of us to prove that this is the principle upon which all eternity has acted and will act; for every reflecting mind must know that it is by reason of this power that all the hosts of heaven perform their works of wonder, majesty, and glory. Angels move from place to place by virtue of this power; it is by reason of it that they are enabled to descend from heaven to earth; and were it not for the power of faith they never could be ministering spirits to them who should be heirs of salvation, neither could they act as heavenly messengers, for they would be destitute of the power necessary to enable them to do the will of God.

5. It is only necessary for us to say that the whole visible creation, as it now exists, is the effect of faith. It was faith by which it was framed, and it is by the power of faith that it continues in its organized form, and by which the planets move round their orbits and sparkle forth their glory. So, then, faith is truly the first principle in the science of THEOLOGY, and, when understood, leads the mind back to the beginning, and carries it forward to the end; or, in other words, from eternity to eternity.

6. As faith, then, is the principle by which the heavenly hosts perform their works, and by which they enjoy all their felicity, we might expect to find it set forth in a revelation from God as the principle upon which his creatures here below must act in

---

19. Genesis 1:3; Joshua 10:12–13; 1 Kings 17:1; 18:1, 41–45. See Matthew 17:20; Luke 17:6.

order to obtain the felicities enjoyed by the saints in the eternal world; and that, when God would undertake to raise up men for the enjoyment of himself, he would teach them the necessity of living by faith, and the impossibility there was of their enjoying the blessedness of eternity without it, seeing that all the blessings of eternity are the effects of faith.

7. Therefore it is said, and appropriately too, that "Without faith it is impossible to please God."[20] If it should be asked— Why is it impossible to please God without faith? The answer would be—Because without faith it is impossible for men to be saved; and as God desires the salvation of men, he must, of course, desire that they should have faith; and he could not be pleased unless they had, or else he could be pleased with their destruction.

8. From this we learn that the many exhortations which have been given by inspired men, to those who had received the word of the Lord to have faith in him, were not mere common-place matters, but were for the best of all reasons, and that was— because without it there was no salvation, neither in this world nor in that which is to come. When men begin to live by faith they begin to draw near to God; and when faith is perfected they are like him; and because he is saved they are saved also; for they will be in the same situation he is in, because they have come to him; and when he appears they shall be like him, for they will see him as he is.

9. As all the visible creation is an effect of faith, so is salvation also—we mean salvation in its most extensive latitude of inter- pretation, whether it is temporal or spiritual. In order to have this subject clearly set before the mind, let us ask what situa- tion must a person be in in order to be saved? or what is the difference between a saved man and one who is not saved? We answer, from what we have before seen of the heavenly worlds, they must be persons who can work by faith and who are able, by faith, to be ministering spirits to them who shall be heirs of salvation; and they must have faith to enable them to act in the

---

20. See Hebrews 11:6.

presence of the Lord, otherwise they cannot be saved. And what constitutes the real difference between a saved person and one not saved is—the difference in the degree of their faith—one's faith has become perfect enough to lay hold upon eternal life, and the other's has not. But to be a little more particular, let us ask—Where shall we find a prototype into whose likeness we may be assimilated, in order that we may be made partakers of life and salvation? or, in other words, where shall we find a saved being? for if we can find a saved being, we may ascertain without much difficulty what all others must be in order to be saved. We think that it will not be a matter of dispute, that two beings who are unlike each other cannot both be saved; for whatever constitutes the salvation of one will constitute the salvation of every creature which will be saved; and if we find one saved being in all existence, we may see what all others must be, or else not be saved. We ask, then, where is the prototype? or where is the saved being? We conclude, as to the answer of this question, there will be no dispute among those who believe the bible, that it is Christ: all will agree in this, that he is the prototype or standard of salvation; or, in other words, that he is a saved being. And if we should continue our interrogation, and ask how it is that he is saved? the answer would be—because he is a just and holy being; and if he were anything different from what he is he would not be saved; for his salvation depends on his being precisely what he is and nothing else; for if it were possible for him to change, in the least degree, so sure he would fail of salvation and lose all his dominion, power, authority and glory, which constitute salvation; for salvation consists in the glory, authority, majesty, power and dominion which Jehovah possesses and in nothing else; and no being can possess it but himself or one like him. Thus says John, in his first epistle, third chapter, second and third verses: "Beloved, now are we the sons of God, and it doth not yet appear what we shall be; but we know that, when he shall appear, we shall be like him, for we shall see him as he is. And every man that hath this hope in him purifieth himself, even as he is pure." Why purify themselves as he is pure? Because if they do not they cannot be like him.

10. The Lord said unto Moses, Leviticus 19:2: "Speak unto all the congregation of the children of Israel, and say unto them, Ye shall be holy: for I the Lord your God am holy." And Peter says, first epistle [of Peter], 1:15–16: "But as he which hath called you is holy, so be ye holy in all manner of conversation; because it is written, Be ye holy; for I am holy." And the Saviour says, Matthew 5:48: "Be ye therefore perfect, even as your Father which is in heaven is perfect." If any should ask, why all these sayings? the answer is to be found from what is before quoted from John's epistle, that when he (the Lord) shall appear, the saints will be like him; and if they are not holy, as he is holy, and perfect, as he is perfect, they cannot be like him; for no being can enjoy his glory without possessing his perfections and holiness, no more than they could reign in his kingdom without his power.

11. This clearly sets forth the propriety of the Saviour's saying, recorded in John's testimony, 14:12: "Verily, verily, I say unto you, He that believeth on me, the works that I do shall he do also; and greater works than these shall he do; because I go unto my Father." This taken in connection with some of the sayings in the Saviour's prayer, recorded in the seventeenth chapter, gives great clearness to his expressions. He says in the 20th to 24th verses: "Neither pray I for these alone, but for them also which shall believe on me through their word; that they all may be one; as thou, Father, art in me, and I in thee, that they also may be one in us: that the world may believe that thou hast sent me. And the glory which thou gavest me I have given them; that they may be one, even as we are one: I in them, and thou in me, that they may be made perfect in one; and that the world may know that thou hast sent me, and hast loved them, as thou hast loved me. Father, I will that they also, whom thou hast given me, be with me where I am; that they may behold my glory, which thou hast given me: for thou lovedst me before the foundation of the world."

12. All these sayings put together give as clear an account of the state of the glorified saints as language could give—the works that Jesus had done they were to do, and greater works than those which he had done among them should they do, and

that because he went to the Father. He does not say that they should do these works in time; but they should do greater works, because he went to the Father. He says in the 24th verse: "Father, I will that they also, whom thou hast given me, be with me where I am; that they may behold my glory." These sayings, taken in connection, make it very plain that the greater works which those that believed on his name were to do were to be done in eternity, where he was going and where they should behold his glory. He had said, in another part of his prayer, that he desired of his Father that those who believed on him should be one in him, as he and the Father were one in each other. "Neither pray I for these [the apostles] alone, but for them also which shall believe on me through their word; that they all may be one"; that is, they who believe on him through the apostles' words, as well as the apostles themselves, "that they all may be one; as thou, Father, art in me and I in thee, that they also may be one in us."[21]

13. What language can be plainer than this? The Saviour surely intended to be understood by his disciples, and he so spake that they might understand him; for he declares to his Father, in language not to be easily mistaken, that he wanted his disciples, even all of them, to be as himself and the Father, for as he and the Father were one so they might be one with them. And what is said in the 22nd verse is calculated to more firmly establish this belief, if it needs anything to establish it. He says: "And the glory which thou gavest me I have given them; that they may be one, even as we are one." As much as to say that unless they have the glory which the Father had given him they could not be one with them; for he says he had given them the glory that the Father had given him that they might be one; or, in other words, to make them one.

14. This fills up the measure of information on this subject, and shows most clearly that the Saviour wished his disciples to understand that they were to be partakers with him in all things, not even his glory excepted.

---

21. John 17:20–21.

15. It is scarcely necessary here to observe what we have previously noticed, that the glory which the Father and the Son have is because they are just and holy beings; and that if they were lacking in one attribute or perfection which they have, the glory which they have never could be enjoyed by them, for it requires them to be precisely what they are in order to enjoy it; and if the Saviour gives this glory to any others, he must do it in the very way set forth in his prayer to his Father—by making them one with him as he and the Father are one. In so doing he would give them the glory which the Father has given him; and when his disciples are made one with the Father and Son, as the Father and the Son are one, who cannot see the propriety of the Saviour's saying—"The works that I do shall he do also; and greater works than these shall he do; because I go unto my Father."[22]

16. These teachings of the Saviour most clearly show unto us the nature of salvation, and what he proposed unto the human family when he proposed to save them—that he proposed to make them like unto himself, and he was like the Father, the great prototype of all saved beings; and for any portion of the human family to be assimilated into their likeness is to be saved; and to be unlike them is to be destroyed; and on this hinge turns the door of salvation.

17. Who cannot see, then, that salvation is the effect of faith? for, as we have previously observed, all the heavenly beings work by this principle; and it is because they are able so to do that they are saved, for nothing but this could save them. And this is the lesson which the God of heaven, by the mouth of all his holy prophets, has been endeavouring to teach to the world. Hence we are told, that "Without faith it is impossible to please God";[23] and that salvation "is of faith, that it might be by grace; to the end the promise might be sure to all the seed." (Romans 4:16.) And that Israel, who followed after the law of righteousness, has not attained to the law of righteousness. "Wherefore? Because they sought it not by faith, but as it

---

22. John 14:12.
23. Hebrews 11:6.

were by the works of the law. For they stumbled at that stumblingstone." (Romans 9:32.) And Jesus said unto the man who brought his son to him, to get the devil who tormented him cast out: "If thou canst believe, all things are possible to him that believeth." (Mark 9:23.) These with a multitude of other scriptures which might be quoted plainly set forth the light in which the Saviour, as well as the Former-day Saints, viewed the plan of salvation. That it was a system of faith—it begins with faith, and continues by faith; and every blessing which is obtained in relation to it is the effect of faith, whether it pertains to this life or that which is to come. To this all the revelations of God bear witness. If there were children of promise, they were the effects of faith, not even the Saviour of the world excepted. "Blessed is she that believed," said Elizabeth to Mary, when she went to visit her, "for there shall be a performance of those things which were told her from the Lord." (Luke 1:45.) Nor was the birth of John the Baptist the less a matter of faith; for in order that his father Zacharias might believe he was struck dumb. And through the whole history of the scheme of life and salvation, it is a matter of faith: every man received according to his faith—according as his faith was, so were his blessings and privileges; and nothing was withheld from him when his faith was sufficient to receive it. He could stop the mouths of lions, quench the violence of fire, escape the edge of the sword, wax valiant in fight, and put to flight the armies of the aliens; women could, by their faith, receive their dead children to life again; in a word, there was nothing impossible with them who had faith. All things were in subjection to the Former-day Saints, according as their faith was. By their faith they could obtain heavenly visions, the ministering of angels, have knowledge of the spirits of just men made perfect, of the general assembly and church of the first born, whose names are written in heaven, of God the judge of all, of Jesus the Mediator of the new covenant, and become familiar with the third heavens, see and hear things which were not only unutterable, but were unlawful to utter. Peter, in view of the power of faith, second epistle [of Peter], first chapter, second and third verses, says to the Former-day Saints: "Grace and peace be multiplied unto you, through the knowledge of God, and of Jesus our Lord, according as his divine power hath given unto us all things that pertain unto life and godliness, through the knowledge of him that hath called us to glory and virtue." In the first epistle [of Peter], first chapter, third to fifth verses, he says: "Blessed be the God and Father of our Lord Jesus Christ, which according to his abundant mercy hath begotten us again unto a lively hope by the resurrection of Jesus Christ from the dead, to an inheritance incorruptible and undefiled, and that fadeth not away, reserved in heaven for you, who are kept by the power of God through faith unto salvation ready to be revealed in the last time."

18. These sayings put together show the apostle's views most clearly, so as to admit of no mistake on the mind of any individual. He says that all things that pertain to life and godliness were given unto them through the knowledge of God and our Saviour Jesus Christ. And if the question is asked, how were they to obtain the knowledge of God? (for there is a great difference between believing in God and knowing him—knowledge implies more than faith. And notice, that all things that pertain to life and godliness were given through the knowledge of God) the answer is given—through faith they were to obtain this knowledge; and, having power by faith to obtain the knowledge of God, they could with it obtain all other things which pertain to life and godliness.

19. By these sayings of the apostle, we learn that it was by obtaining a knowledge of God that men got the knowledge of all things which pertain to life and godliness, and this knowledge was the effect of faith; so that all things which pertain to life and godliness are the effects of faith.

20. From this we may extend as far as any circumstances may require, whether on earth or in heaven, and we will find it the testimony of all inspired men, or heavenly messengers, that all things that pertain to life and godliness are the effects of faith and nothing else; all learning, wisdom and prudence fail, and every thing else as a means of salvation but faith. This is the reason that the fishermen of Galilee could teach the world—because they sought by faith, and by faith obtained. And this is the reason that Paul counted all things but filth and dross—what he

formerly called his gain he called his loss; yea, and he counted all things but loss for the excellency of the knowledge of Christ Jesus the Lord.[24] Because to obtain the faith by which he could enjoy the knowledge of Christ Jesus the Lord, he had to suffer the loss of all things. This is the reason that the Former-day Saints knew more, and understood more, of heaven and of heavenly things than all others beside, because this information is the effect of faith—to be obtained by no other means. And this is the reason that men, as soon as they lose their faith, run into strifes, contentions, darkness, and difficulties; for the knowledge which tends to life disappears with faith, but returns when faith returns; for when faith comes it brings its train of attendants with it—apostles, prophets, evangelists, pastors, teachers, gifts, wisdom, knowledge, miracles, healings, tongues, interpretation of tongues, etc. All these appear when faith appears on the earth, and disappear when it disappears from the earth; for these are the effects of faith, and always have attended, and always will, attend it. For where faith is, there will the knowledge of God be also, with all things which pertain thereto—revelations, visions, and dreams, as well as every necessary thing, in order that the possessors of faith may be perfected, and obtain salvation; for God must change, otherwise faith will prevail with him. And he who possesses it will, through it, obtain all necessary knowledge and wisdom, until he shall know God, and the Lord Jesus Christ, whom he has sent—whom to know is eternal life. Amen.

---

24. Philippians 3:7–10.

Man's Destiny

Lorenzo Snow

Before his baptism into the Church, Lorenzo Snow attended a meeting in the Kirtland Temple, where he listened to several patriarchal blessings given by Joseph Smith Sr., father of the Prophet. After the meeting, Lorenzo was introduced to the Patriarch, who predicted that the young man would soon be baptized. He also told him, "You will become as great as you can possibly wish—EVEN AS GREAT AS GOD, and you cannot wish to be greater." (Eliza R. Snow, *Biography and Family Record of Lorenzo Snow* [Salt Lake City: Deseret News, 1884], 10.)

Lorenzo later wrote, "The old gentleman's prediction, that I should ere long be baptized, was strange to me, for I had not cherished a thought of becoming a member of the 'Mormon' Church; but when he uttered the last clause, I was confounded. That, to me, was a big saying, and, I then thought, approaching almost to blasphemy. And why not? After years of study and diligent search after knowledge, in that which most intimately concerned me—'From whence came I?' 'Why am I here?' 'What is my future destiny?' In all this, I was profoundly ignorant. As yet I had received no key that could unlock those mysteries—that could make known, to my satisfaction, my relationship to Him who controls the universe.

"I looked at Father Smith, and silently asked myself the question: Can that man be a deceiver? His every appearance answered in the negative. At first sight, his presence impressed me with feelings of love and reverence. I had never seen age so prepossessing. Father Joseph Smith, the Patriarch, was indeed a noble specimen of aged manhood.

"But with all my favorable impressions of the Patriarch, that *big saying* was a dark parable. The prediction that I should soon be baptized was fulfilled in two weeks from the time it was spoken, and in about four years from that time I was reminded of the foregoing prediction by a very wonderful revelation on the subject in which the principle, as well as the promise, was made clear to my understanding as the sun at noonday." (Ibid.)

Brother Snow wrote the essence of that revelation as a couplet, which has become well-known in the Church:

> As man now is, God once was;
> As God now is, man may be.

Less well-known is the fact that on January 11, 1892, he wrote a poem, "Man's Destiny," on the same subject. The poem is addressed to the Apostle Paul in response to Philippians 2:5–6: "Let this mind be in you, which was also in Christ Jesus, who, being in the form of God, thought it not robbery to be equal with God." The poem also refers to 1 John 3:2–3: "Beloved, now are we the sons of God, and it doth not yet appear what we shall be: but we know that, when he shall appear, we shall be like him; for we shall see him as he is. And every man that hath this hope in him purifieth himself, even as he is pure."

Dear Brother:

> Hast thou not been unwisely bold,
> Man's destiny to thus unfold?
> To raise, promote such high desire,
> Such vast ambition thus inspire?
> Still, 'tis no phantom that we trace
> Man's ultimatum in life's race;
> This royal path has long been trod
> By righteous men, each now a God:

Man's Destiny

As Abra'm, Isaac, Jacob, too,
First babes, then men—to gods they grew.
As man now is, our God once was;
As now God is, so man may be,—
Which doth unfold man's destiny.
For John declares: When Christ we see
Like unto him we'll truly be.
And he who has this hope within,
Will purify himself from sin.
Who keep this object grand in view,
To folly, sin, will bid adieu,
Nor wallow in the mire anew;
Nor ever seek to carve his name
High on the shaft of worldly fame;
But here his ultimatum trace:
The head of all his spirit-race.
Ah, well: that taught by you, dear Paul,
'Though much amazed, we see it all;
Our Father God, has ope'd our eyes,
We cannot view it otherwise.
The boy, like to his father grown,
Has but attained unto his own;
To grow to sire from state of son,
Is not 'gainst Nature's course to run.
A son of God, like God to be,
Would not be robbing Deity;
And he who has this hope within,
Will purify himself from sin.
You're right, St. John, supremely right:
Whoe'er essays to climb this height,
Will cleanse himself of sin entire—
Or else 'twere needless to aspire.

—*Improvement Era,* June 1919, 660–61.

Invocation, or the Eternal Father and Mother

Eliza R. Snow

Elder Bruce R. McConkie wrote, "Implicit in the Christian verity that all men are the spirit children of an *Eternal Father* is the usually unspoken truth that they are also the offspring of an *Eternal Mother.* This glorious truth of celestial parentage, including specifically both a Father and a Mother,[1] is heralded forth by song in one of the greatest of Latter-day Saint hymns, *O My Father,* by Eliza R. Snow." (*Mormon Doctrine*, 2d ed. [Salt Lake City: Bookcraft, 1966], 516–17.)

George D. Pyper, in his book *Stories of Latter-day Saint Hymns,* wrote, "Zina D. Huntington [a close friend of the Prophet Joseph and of Eliza R. Snow] . . . was grieved over an unusual circumstance. Her mother, who had died some time before, had been buried in a temporary grave, and it became necessary to remove the body to a permanent resting place. When the remains were exhumed it was discovered that they were partially petrified. It

---

1. This doctrine was also taught by the First Presidency in "The Origin of Man," included in this book ("Man, as a spirit, was begotten and born of heavenly parents"; "All men and women are in the similitude of the universal Father and Mother, and are literally the sons and daughters of Deity") and in 1995 by the First Presidency and Council of the Twelve in "The Family: A Proclamation to the World": "All human beings—male and female—are created in the image of God. Each is a beloved spirit son or daughter of heavenly parents, and, as such, each has a divine nature and destiny. Gender is an essential characteristic of individual premortal, mortal, and eternal identity and purpose."

seemed to Zina as if the very foundation of the doctrine of the resurrection crumbled. To the question 'Shall I know my mother when I meet her in the world beyond?' the Prophet responded emphatically, 'Yes, you will know your mother there.' A firm believer in Joseph's divine mission, Zina D. Huntington was comforted by the promise. From the discussions on the resurrection and the relationship of man to Deity no doubt came the inspiration to Eliza R. Snow for the writing of 'O My Father.' . . .

"The hymn is in four stanzas and is an epitome of the great drama of eternal life as revealed by the restored Gospel of Jesus Christ.

"The Prologue: The first stanza proclaims the literal Fatherhood of God; that we were nurtured by His side in our antemortal existence, connoting the truth that we were instructed in the great plan, obedience to which would enable us to regain His presence 'and again behold His face.'

"The Play: Stanza II shifts the scene to earth-life, where we are placed in a school to see whether we will do the things required of us and prove our right to the promised restoration to God's presence. Our recollection of ante-mortal life is withheld in order that we may walk by faith; yet, not to be left wholly in the dark, a 'secret something,' a key that opens the door to knowledge, is given us, and through it (Stanza III) is revealed the new and glorious doctrine that we are children of a Mother in heaven.

"The Epilogue: Back again into the Eternal Presence our thoughts are projected. Through obedience, and through having competed all we have been commanded to do, with the 'mutual approbation' of our heavenly Parents, we claim the promise made in our ante-mortal state.

"Truly 'O My Father' is the drama of eternal life: not merely a hymn, but a prophecy and a revelation." ([Salt Lake City: Deseret News Press, 1939], 4-6.)

O my Father, thou that dwellest
In the high and glorious place,
When shall I regain thy presence,

And again behold thy face?
In thy holy habitation,
Did my spirit once reside?
In my first primeval childhood,
Was I nurtured near thy side?

For a wise and glorious purpose
Thou hast placed me here on earth,
And withheld the recollection
Of my former friends and birth.
Yet ofttimes a secret something
Whispered, "You're a stranger here."
And I felt that I had wandered
From a more exalted sphere.

I had learned to call thee Father,
Through thy Spirit from on high;
But until the key of knowledge
Was restored, I knew not why.
In the heavens are parents single?
No; the thought makes reason stare!
Truth is reason, truth eternal
Tells me I've a mother there.

When I leave this frail existence,
When I lay this mortal by,
Father, Mother, may I meet you
In your royal courts on high?
Then, at length, when I've completed
All you sent me forth to do,
With your mutual approbation
Let me come and dwell with you.

—*Hymns* (Salt Lake City: The Church of Jesus Christ
of Latter-day Saints, 1985), no. 292.

Made in the USA
Las Vegas, NV
12 February 2022